The Triumph of Horus

THE TRIUMPH OF HORUS

AN ANCIENT EGYPTIAN SACRED DRAMA

translated and edited by

H. W. FAIRMAN

Brunner Professor of Egyptology, University of Liverpool

with a chapter by DEREK NEWTON *Head of Department*
and DEREK POOLE *Principal Lecturer*

Department of Drama in Education and Theatre Craft
Padgate College of Education

B. T. BATSFORD LTD · *LONDON*

To MY WIFE with love and gratitude

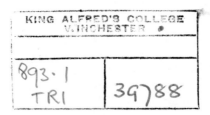
First published 1974
© H. W. Fairman 1974
Chapter 3 © Derek Newton and Derek Poole 1974

Made and printed in Great Britain by
C. Tinling & Co Ltd, Prescot
for the publishers B. T. Batsford Ltd
4 Fitzhardinge Street, London W.1

ISBN 0 7134 1983 0

Contents

Preface

The Triumph of Horus was first published in an English translation, accompanied by a detailed commentary, by the late Professor A. M. Blackman and myself in the *Journal of Egyptian Archaeology*, volumes 28, 29 and 30 in the years 1942–1944. In the intervening years our basic translation has remained, and still remains, substantially unchanged in all essentials. Nevertheless, the form in which the play appears in this book is entirely new. A brief outline of how this has come about may not be out of place.

It was about 1933 that I first began seriously to prepare translations of the five texts at Edfu that make up what we are now accustomed to call the Myth of Horus. The first article, The Legend of the Winged Disk (Myth A), was published in 1935. I had already recognised and announced the dramatic nature of *The Triumph of Horus* (Myth C) and was working on a translation and commentary but, as by this time Professor Blackman and I had embarked on the preparation of a series of studies of Ptolemaic texts, I suggested that the rest of the Myth of Horus should be published as our joint work.

At this time the material consisted of a complete draft translation of *The Triumph of Horus* in which the main text was set out as a play and a preliminary, but very incomplete, collection of notes and material for the commentary. My draft translation needed little serious change, except that the precise style and wording gained immeasurably from Professor Blackman's unique gift of expression in English.

I also submitted a tentative and embryonic scheme for the embodiment of the short texts accompanying the reliefs into the main text, which we both agreed was a play. I was already inclined to suspect that reliefs and main text could not be divorced. This scheme was not adopted: it was rather revolutionary and my older and more cautious friend felt that in an *editio princeps* we ought to be completely honest and keep main texts and reliefs separate.

I accepted this decision but have always regretted it. The result, in fact, was that the true significance and purpose was almost completely obscured or lost and even its dramatic nature was impaired. Since those days my own researches into Ptolemaic texts and certain aspects of

Egyptian archaeology and religion have widened and deepened and what in 1935 was little more than a feeling has become a conviction. Thus I have reverted to my original view and in the version of the play printed in this book the reliefs and the main text have been combined into a single composition. The reasons for this new form and the rules that have governed the reconstruction of the play in its new shape are given and discussed in Chapter 2.

The second way in which the play now diverges from our original version is in the attempt to set it out as verse. There is, I feel, a very strong probability that the play was in verse but the exact form in which it is printed is frankly experimental. I have been denied the time and opportunity to submit the verse form to the research and critical study that I desired. The verse form is merely an experiment, imperfect, that is certainly capable of considerable improvement. The translation itself is unaffected by this and is as accurate as one can make it.

The translation is virtually unchanged. I have retained our very deliberate and planned diction and vocabulary but its 'Biblical' flavour has been somewhat modified. The whole text has been carefully and repeatedly checked and revised; a few minor improvements have been incorporated; at least one desperately damaged passage, which had previously defeated all attempts at interpretation, has been deciphered and translated. Since the printed text was prepared initially for a stage production and for the general reader all lacunae have been omitted (they are relatively few) and all diacritical points and marks and most brackets and question marks have been eliminated. The exact state of the text, apart from new readings, is meticulously indicated in our original publication.

The accident by which this play came to be produced and acted is described in Chapter 3. It was an indescribable experience on 23 June 1971 to witness the bringing to life of this long-lost play. I was, and remain, filled with admiration for the skill, imagination and integrity displayed by Mr Newton and all his staff in their pioneering production. My admiration for, and gratitude to, the students of the Department of Drama at Padgate College of Education is unbounded: they had to unlearn most of the lessons they had been taught, cope with a strange and very difficult vocabulary and undergo enormous physical strain: *Horus* owes them a very great debt.

I am also indebted to many others. In particular to Dr Serge Sauneron, Director of the Institut Français d'Archéologie Orientale, Cairo, for permission to use E. Chassinat, *Le Temple d' Edfou*, X, pls. CXLVI–CXLVIII for the line drawings reproduced as figures 6–16, 18 and 19.

I am also grateful to my student, Mr A. J. Spencer, for his patience and skill in drawing figures 4 and 17: figure 4 is based essentially on M. Alliot, *Rapport sur les fouilles de Tell Edfou 1933*, pl. xx, and *Le Culte d' Horus à Edfou au temps des Ptolémées*, II, pl. IV, with certain modifications embodying my own ideas and opinions.

Last and most important I am grateful beyond words to my wife for her skill and patience in typing the whole book and coping with the awkward and refractory manuscript presented to her.

List of Plates

List of figures in the text

1 *Drama in Ancient Egypt*

The problem whether there *was* drama in Egypt is notoriously difficult to solve and views for and against have been put forward and contested with equal vigour and dogmatism. The difficulties are genuine and stem partly from the fact that no specialised Ancient Egyptian building that could be identified as a theatre has ever been found, and it is extremely improbable that one ever existed, and partly from the nature of the Egyptian writing and texts and the total absence of a single document that is clearly labelled as a play; we do not even know whether the Egyptians had words for 'drama', play', 'act' or 'scene'.

The writings of the classical authors on the subject of the Egyptian 'mysteries', especially those of Osiris, have often been cited as proof that there must have been dramatic performances and dramas in Egypt. The most celebrated of these is the passage in which Herodotus describes certain ceremonies at Papremis[1]:

> But at Papremis, besides the sacrifices and other rites which were performed there as elsewhere, the following custom is observed: When the sun is getting low, a few only of the priests continue occupied about the image of the god, while the greater number, armed with wooden clubs, take their station at the portal of the temple. Opposite to them is drawn up a body of men, in number above a thousand, armed, like the others, with clubs, consisting of persons engaged in the performance of their vows. The image of the god, which is kept in a small wooden shrine covered with plates of gold, is conveyed from the temple into a second sacred building the day before the festival begins. The few priests still in attendance upon the image place it, together with the shrine containing it, on a four-wheeled car, and begin to drag it along; the others, stationed at the gateway of the temple oppose its admission. Then the votaries come forward to espouse the quarrel of the god, and set upon the opponents, who are sure to offer resistance. A sharp fight with clubs ensues, in which heads are commonly broken on both sides. Many, I am convinced, die of wounds that they received, though the Egyptians insist that no one is ever killed.

A passage more nearly contemporary with Herodotus than any hieroglyphic document yet known occurs in a stela of the Graeco-Roman Period now in the Cairo Museum[2]:

Ye who come from the Meadow of the God, when the plants become verdant, in order to worship at the Festival of Horus, who speed to (aid) Min when he goes forth to his dais, drawn by horses, adorned with red cloth and equipped with a pectoral, all those before his dais trembling at seeing him in danger, but when he emerges safely, the faint hearted, who was inactive, seizes his spear and attacks his adversaries to give subjects to Him-whose-heart-is-tired. ('Him-whose-heart-is-tired' is a well-known name of Osiris.)

An even earlier testimony to a similar situation is found in the stela of a certain Ikhernofret who lived in the Twelfth Dynasty in the reign of Sesostris III[3]:

I arrayed the god in his regalia in my office of Chief-of-the-Mysteries, in my capacity of *Sma*-priest. I was one pure of hand in adorning the god, a *sem*-priest pure of fingers. I performed the Going-forth of Wepwawet when he set forth to protect his father. I drove back the rebels from the *neshmet*-bark (the sacred bark of Osiris), I overthrew the enemies of Osiris. I performed the Great Going-forth. I followed the God in his journeyings. I caused the sacred bark to voyage, Thoth directing the journey. I equipped the bark 'Appearing in Truth' of the Lord of Abydos (Osiris) with a cabin: its beautiful adornments were affixed when he proceeded to U-peker. I directed the paths of the god to his tomb in Peker. I protected Onnophris on that day of the great combat. I overthrew all his enemies upon the bank of Nedyet.

The stela of Ikhernofret has been interpreted as recording the mysteries of Osiris and the enactment of episodes in his life. All three sources stress actions that took place when the processional bark of a god was carried in procession on the shoulders of priests and when it was attacked by men impersonating the enemies of the god and defended by others of his devotees. There is no hint here of a formal play with words and we seem to have, rather, mimed actions during the procession of a god in which there is certainly a definite 'dramatic' element, a public and popular display but scarcely a play in itself.

It has also been claimed that there must have been drama in Ancient Egypt because so many rituals, festivals and even the daily temple ritual itself incorporated so many dramatic elements. The daily temple ritual is admitted to be a kind of dramatisation on the religious plane of the average day of the average human. The daily temple ritual consists essentially of three services, at dawn, midday and sunset. The morning service is the longest and most important and when stripped to its bare essentials consists of the awakening of the god, his undressing, bathing, anointing, dressing, investment with his regalia and feeding. The midday service is much briefer; the evening service was more elaborate but not, apparently, as important as the morning service. These three services may easily be equated in terms of human life with waking from sleep, bathing and dressing, and breakfast; with the light noon collation and the heavier evening meal before going to bed. Similarly the great festivals and the appearances of the god daily and throughout the year may be equated with the activities of any king or senior official. This is true but there is nowhere any hint that these daily services were themselves conceived, planned or acted as dramas; they were dramatisations of the episodes of daily life but in no way were they plays.

Before 1928 this was the utmost that could be said about drama in Egypt. There was always the possibility that drama existed but no play or fragment of a play could be quoted with any certainty. It was in 1928 that the great German scholar Kurt Sethe published his *Dramatische Texte zu altägyptischen Mysterienspielen*[4] in which he presented the text, translation and commentary on what he claimed were two very ancient plays.

The first of these documents is one of the most famous and most important of all hieroglyphic texts and is commonly cited as either the Memphite Theology or the Shabaka Stone. It is found on a block of granite which for over a century has been in the British Museum and which had already been studied and translated (a full bibliography is given by Sethe) before Sethe published his edition. The surviving text had been piously carved by orders of Shabaka, a king of the Twenty-fifth (Ethiopian) Dynasty (715–702 B.C.) in order to preserve a more ancient manuscript. It had probably been erected originally in the Temple of Ptah at Memphis but was found in Cairo and in its long life had acted as mill stone and as threshold of a door, as a result of which very large sections have been irretrievably lost. Sethe considered that the original text should be assigned to the First Dynasty. This extreme view cannot be sustained. In subsequent studies Hermann Junker[5] demonstrated that the text could be divided into two sections, a political teaching (lines 3–44) and a religious teaching (lines 45–58); it is the former that contains the dramatic text. Junker considered it impossible to suggest a precise date but favoured the early Old Kingdom.

The whole inscription is propaganda in favour of Ptah of Memphis in opposition to the rising power and influence of Re and the priesthood of Heliopolis. The political (dramatic) section claims that Ptah-Tanen is the King of Egypt and Memphis the capital of the Two Lands; it describes how Geb sought to end the conflict between Horus and Seth by assigning Lower Egypt to Horus and Upper Egypt to Seth and then reversed his decision and assigned the whole land to Horus as legitimate heir, but Horus in reality was none other than Ptah-Tanen; Memphis is the place where the Two Lands were united and where Osiris was buried, and the royal palace in Memphis is the visible sign of the union. In the religious teaching the supremacy of Ptah over the whole creation is the theme: all the great gods are only hypostases of Ptah who even created the Ennead (the Heliopolitan theological system), and the entire creation was produced by the thought of his mind and the word of his tongue, and thus also the moral order was founded.

The whole text is written in vertical columns. These, however, in the dramatic sections show certain peculiarities. Portions of the text are pure narrative but in those sections that contain dialogue the speaker and the person addressed are indicated by writing their names facing each other over the phrase 'words to be recited', the latter always being written in the same direction as the name of the speaker.

Thus a grouping

$$\longrightarrow \qquad \longleftarrow$$

Geb   Horus

$$\overline{\longrightarrow}$$

Words to be recited

is to be translated 'Geb said to Horus.' The speeches are also interrupted by horizontal rulings creating one or more cases in which are written, by way of explanation, the name of a god and sometimes an additional word. To illustrate the text and its composition we give a translation of the best preserved portion, which deals with Geb's attempts to pacify Horus and Seth. The vertical lines in the translation indicate the rulings in the original.

Geb, Prince of the Gods commanded that the Ennead should assemble around him

He separated Horus and Seth

He forbade them to quarrel.

He placed Seth as Upper Egyptian King in Upper Egypt, to the place in which he was born, in Su.

And Geb he placed Horus as Lower Egyptian King in Lower Egypt, to the place in which his father was drowned, in Peseshet-towi.

Thus Horus stood over (one) place.

Thus Seth stood over the (other) place.

They were in concord over the Two Lands in Ayan: it was the boundary of the Two Lands

Geb said to Seth: 'Go to the place in which you were born' | Seth | Upper Egypt |

Geb said to Horus: 'Go to the place where your father was drowned.' | Horus | Lower Egypt |

Geb said to Horus and Seth: 'I have separated you' | — | Lower Egypt, Upper Egypt |

It was painful to the heart of Geb that the portion of Horus should be like the portion of Seth.

Thus Geb gave his (whole) inheritance to Horus—he is the son of his son, his first born

Geb said to the Ennead: I have appointed (*lit.* commanded) | Horus | thee to be successor,

„ „ „ „ „   thou alone. | Horus. | The inheritance

„ „ „ „ „   belongs to that heir. | Horus | My inheritance

„ „ „ „ „   belongs to the son of my son, | Horus | the Upper Egyptian jackal

„ „ „ „ „   (my) first-born | Horus | the Opener-of-the-way

„ „ „ „ „   he is the son, who was born | Horus | when the Opener of the Way was born.

Horus stood over the land. He is the Uniter of this land, who is named with the great name 'Tanen, Who-is-south-of-his-wall, Lord of Eternity.'

The Two Great-of-Magic grew on his head. He is Horus who has appeared as King of Upper and Lower Egypt, who has united the Two Lands in Memphis in the place in which the Two Lands were united.

The second text published by Sethe, the Ramesseum Dramatic Papyrus, is a papyrus of the Middle Kingdom found at the Ramesseum by Quibell in his excavations of 1895/6. The text is written in 138 vertical columns which in organisation are similar to the Shabaka Stone and show the same method of indicating the speakers and the same subdivision of the columns into smaller cases. In contrast with the Shabaka Stone, however, there is a series of 31 vignettes the whole breadth of the papyrus below the columns of text.

Sethe interpreted the papyrus as the Coronation Ritual of Sesostris I (1971–1928 B.C.) and this was for long accepted without serious questioning, though it has been realised that Sethe's interpretation involves certain difficulties and inconsistencies. Two recent studies by Helck[6] and Altenmüller[7] have shed new light on the nature and purpose of the papyrus. It now appears that the papyrus in its present form and arrangement does not represent the original order of the text: the prototype had through hard use and folding broken into fragments which had been reassembled in a wrong order by an ancient scribe. A new order of the text has thus been obtained. The modern arguments and the consequential rearranging of the text appear to be convincing and correct. The result is that the text can no longer be accepted as a Coronation Ritual but is a ritual play for the Jubilee (Heb-sed) of Sesostris I. It is interesting to note that though the papyrus bears the name of Sesostris I, the surviving version appears to have been written in the reign of Amenemhat III (1841–1794 B.C.), presumably for his Jubilee. This is evidence that the ritual was in regular use for some 200 years: the prototype may well, of course, have been even older.

The papyrus consists of 46 scenes, which it has been suggested fall into fourteen groups. Each scene begins with a short narrative and an explanation: these, it may be assumed, were recited by the Reader. These are followed by a brief dialogue between two or more persons, who are or who represent various divinities, and the king himself who impersonates Horus. The dialogues teem with puns which were considered necessary for the magical potency of the spoken words.

A translation of two consecutive scenes (Scenes 42 and 43 according to the new numbering, corresponding to lines 5–7 and 8–10 of the papyrus) is given here. These scenes form part of the preparations for the departure of a ship which follows immediately the Erection of the Ded-Pillar, the culmination of the Jubilee ceremonies. Words in square brackets are restorations for which there is reasonable authority. The vertical lines indicate the lines dividing the various cases.

SCENE 42

It happened that eight *mensa*-vases were brought to the [prow of the shi]p by the royal relatives. It is Thoth who places Osiris on the [back] of Seth that he may raise him up.

Thoth speaks to Seth: Thou canst not endure (long) under him who is greater than thee. | [Osiris] | Numbering of the elders of [the palace].

Thoth speaks to Osiris: Let not his heart be cool thereby. | [Seth] | Ascending to the sky.

SCENE 43

It happened that a royal ox was cut up. It is Horus who is angry; he takes his Eye, in the capacity of Him-with-the-great-breast, from Thoth who comes (?) as one who empties the Eye at the cutting up of all sacrificial oxen

Isis says to Thoth: It is thy lip that has done it to thee. | Thoth | Cutting up and binding (?) the sacrificial ox, first time.

Isis says to Thoth: Shall thy mouth open? | Thoth | Slaughtering the sacrificial ox.

It will be noted that these two scenes are pure ritual: they contain no dramatic development of a story or a theme, other than the presumably prescribed succession of acts of a specific ritual. There is clearly a narrative section, there is speech, but in these two examples, no dialogue, and the cases apparently indicate one of the actors and contain perhaps a stage direction. The ritual aspect is obviously more dominant than in the extract from the Shabaka Stone translated above.

The third fragment of a similar dramatic text, organised and presented in the same way as the Shabaka Stone and the Ramesseum Dramatic Papyrus, is found in the midst of a longer mythological text in the sarcophagus chamber in the Cenotaph of Sethos I at Abydos.[8] The existing version was engraved in the early Nineteenth Dynasty, but grammar and vocabulary suggest that the prototype was extremely early. No useful purpose would be served by attempting to translate the desperately damaged fragments of this text.

These three texts have been claimed to be the earliest dramatic texts that have come down from Ancient Egypt. They are certainly extremely ancient. It is difficult fairly to assess the exact nature of the Abydos text but the Ramesseum Papyrus is obviously best regarded as an example of ritual or liturgical drama. The 'dramatic' portions of the Shabaka Stone are too incomplete to permit a balanced judgement on the whole, but as far as one can judge from the surviving portions the ritual aspect is not as marked as in the Ramesseum Papyrus and one may perhaps be permitted to doubt whether it is really a drama. It may possibly be better and cautiously defined as a politico-mythological compilation incorporating certain dramatic elements which may perhaps have been derived from a drama now lost or perhaps merely employing dialogue to reinforce the main argument.

Much the same verdict must be passed on the Ritual of the Opening of the Mouth[9], of which many versions exist and whose dramatic nature has been remarked upon. In composition this Ritual is very similar to the texts already mentioned. The 75 scenes of which it is composed are entirely ritual acts and are accompanied by reliefs or vignettes. The scenes vary greatly in length: some contain no speeches at all but the majority incorporate a narrative section, the words of one or more officiants, and sometimes longer hymns or invocations. The Ritual undoubtedly was also an ancient one but it too was no more than a ritual drama.

We cannot leave these early dramatic texts without making brief reference to the possibility of the existence of another early drama. Recent researches into the Pyramid Texts and the establishment of the order in which they are to be read are beginning to yield dividends. In 1953 Joachim Spiegel published a lengthy paper[10] in which he summarised the results of his study of the texts in the Pyramid of King Unas at Saqqarah: Unas was the last king of the Fifth Dynasty and his pyramid was the first to be inscribed, and its texts, the Pyramid Texts, are better preserved than those in any of the later pyramids. It was unfortunate that Spiegel's book[11] was only received when this book was entering its final stages and even more unfortunate that a further study of the Pyramid Texts by Hartwig Altenmüller[12] was not received until the last lines of this book were being typed. Time has not been available to submit these two important works to the critical and comparative study that they obviously merit. A final verdict on the problems raised is thus impossible and only a brief, passing reference can be made here.

The essence of Spiegel's thesis is that the texts of the Pyramid of Unas contain a single ritual. It commences on the right as one enters the entrance passage and continues and develops logically as one goes round the walls of the various chambers until one reaches the entrance passage again. Since some of the texts are inscribed above eye level, Spiegel postulates two rituals, a spoken ritual and a shorter silent ritual: this is disturbing since he claims that the ritual is a form of drama. In Spiegel's view the ritual was performed at night, inside the pyramid, with only six officiants. It begins with the bringing of the body of the dead king into the pyramid, the interment in the sarcophagus and thereafter a lengthy series of ceremonies that restore life to the king. Ultimately the soul of the king emerges from the pyramid to greet the new moon which acts as a boat to ferry the king to his future home in the sky. Altenmüller covers much the same ground as Spiegel and obviously at numerous points reaches different conclusions. In the circumstances it would be premature to hazard an opinion. Spiegel believes that the Unas Ritual is a ritual drama, and certain sections are fairly clearly 'dramatic'. Much that he has to say is seductive but on the other hand many objections and doubts rise to mind. Altenmüller's study is very thorough and methodical and produces solid arguments of real substance. The utmost one might venture to say at present is that Spiegel's thesis is not proven.

For the possibility of there being Egyptian dramatic texts in addition to those already mentioned we are dependent almost exclusively on the researches of the late Etienne Drioton. From 1925 until his death a large part of his research activity was concentrated on the problem of drama in Ancient Egypt and resulted in a book[13] and a long list of articles, most unfortunately repetitious, of which the best and most helpful is his '*Le Théâtre dans l'Ancienne Egypte*'.[14] Drioton was able to claim that a series of texts, in longer inscriptions in which no one had seriously thought of looking, were in reality fragments of dramas lifted from their original context and diverted to other purposes. Some of these dramatic fragments were extremely short, none were very long and none were complete dramas. There may be doubts about the complete accuracy of his translations and his exegesis, but Drioton performed an immensely valuable service in raising again in a stimulating manner the problem of drama in Egypt and in opening the way to new avenues of enquiry.

Drioton first attempted to establish criteria for the identification of dramatic works. There were, he claimed, three such criteria: the placing of the name of a speaker at the head of a speech; the presence of stage directions in the midst of the dialogue; the general nature of the text, grammar, dialogue and in general a non-narrative style. These are certainly valid criteria but that they are the only ones is equally certainly wrong. One can reasonably expect to find in a drama a story, a development of a theme, an element of combat of one kind or another and even character drawing, though in early drama this is not necessarily present.

Even Drioton's three criteria are not absolutes; their presence in a text does not automatically mean that it is a drama. A brief quotation will serve to illustrate the point:

When Kean arrived, he sent for me to his dressing room.
You are rather tall, sir.
Rejoinder: Yes, sir, what do you wish me to do?
Kean: Why, in the library scene, sink gradually on your right knee, with your back to the audience. When I place my hand on your head to curse, mind you keep your eyes fixed on mine.
(No very easy task to look steadily into such eyes.)
Is that all, sir?
Kean: Yes—do whatever you like after that; it will be all the same to me.[15]

This quotation is from an essay in a book of essays on the theatre but, in spite of its style and composition, no one would claim that it is an extract from a play. In attempting to assess the extent to which Drioton's claims to have discovered fragments of long lost dramas are justified it is essential to realise that the marks of a drama cannot be codified as simply as he apparently believed.

By the time of his death Drioton had identified fragments of nine dramatic works. It is not possible to give here an account of each and we give merely Drioton's own title of each fragment. Partial translations and connecting commentary are given in varying degree in his book and the longer articles.

1 *The Birth and Apotheosis of Horus*[16] (see further pp. 10–12 below)

2 *The Misfortunes of a Messenger of Horus*[17]
3 *The Defeat of Apopis*[18]
4 *Isis and the Seven Scorpions*[19]
5 *Horus is Bitten by a Scorpion*[20]
6 *Horus is Bitten by a Scorpion*[21]
7 *The Return of Seth.*[22] This text is dissected by Drioton, rearranged and grouped as three plays: (a) a Heliopolitan version, (b) the version of Geb, (c) the version of Osiris.
8 *The Fight between Thoth and Apopis*[23]
9 Two plays which Drioton imagined were the earliest versions of *The Triumph of Horus:* for discussion and analysis see pp. 20–23 below.

In addition to these, Madame C. Desroches-Noblecourt[24] has suggested that two further fragments might be identified:

10 *Horus Burning in the Desert*[25]
11 *A Nightmare of Horus*[26]

These two fragments are very short and their supposedly dramatic nature is highly problematical.

To what extent are these claims justified? It must be repeated that, with the exception of *The Triumph of Horus*, all these texts are fragments, there is no complete play among them. This fact presents insurmountable obstacles to any fair appraisal, for insufficient has survived to enable anyone to form any idea of the complete work. Drioton was convinced that he had identified fragments of ancient plays. On the other hand, some of his identifications have been disputed;[27] the chances of nos. 4, 5, 6 and 7 being plays are remote—the first three are narrative and no. 7 cannot exist in the form Drioton has suggested. In fact, it has to be confessed that no one of these fragments can be accepted as being incontestably a fragment of a lost play: some have dramatic elements but some are in conflict with Drioton's own criteria. Opinions on material of this nature are inevitably intensely personal and subjective: this does not mean that Drioton's work has been wasted, far from it; it does mean that the case is not proved, either for or against, and much work and more critical work is needed.

Of all the fragments identified by Drioton, no. 1 'The Birth and Apotheosis of Horus' is the one that is most likely to be from a genuine play. Five translations and commentaries, by different authors, have since been published;[28] not one of them sets out the translation as a play and some of the authors do not even mention the dramatic possibilities.

I give my own translation of the complete text and as an experiment have set it out as though it were indeed a play. Square brackets have been used to mark speakers whose names are not explicitly stated.

TITLE

To assume the form of a Falcon

[STAGE DIRECTION]

The lightning having struck (?), the gods are afraid; Isis awakes, pregnant with the seed of her brother Osiris; the woman raises herself, quickly, her heart rejoicing because of the seed of her brother Osiris. She says:

ISIS

O Gods, I am Isis, the sister of Osiris, who weeps over the father of the gods, Osiris who ended the carnage of the Two Lands. His seed is within my womb. I have fashioned the form of a god in the egg, namely the son of the head of the Ennead who shall rule this land, who shall inherit Geb, who shall speak on behalf of his father and who shall kill Seth, the enemy of his father Osiris.

Come ye gods and exercise protection over him within my womb. Know (ye) in your hearts that he is your lord, this god who is in his egg, he who is radiant of form, the lord of the gods. Great is their beauty, the barbs (?) of the two plumes of lapis-lazuli.

RE-ATUM

Ho, says Re-Atum, let your heart be wise, O woman! How do you know that he is a god, lord and heir of the Ennead, for whom you are acting within the egg?

ISIS

I am Isis, more glorious and august than the gods. A god is in this womb of mine; he is the seed of Osiris.

RE-ATUM

Then says Re-Atum: If you are pregnant, you should conceal, O Maiden, from the gods when you bear him whom you have conceived and that he is the seed of Osiris, lest that enemy who slew his father come and break the egg in its immaturity, (namely) he of whom the Great-of-Magic is afraid.

ISIS

Hear this ye gods, said Isis, which Atum, Lord of the Mansion of the Sacred Images, has said. He has decreed for me the protection of my son in my womb, having organised an entourage around him in this uterus of mine, for he knows that he is the heir of Osiris. The guard of the Falcon who is in this womb of mine has been set by Re-Atum, Lord of the Gods.

Come! Come forth on earth that I may give thee praise. The servitors of thy father Osiris will serve thee; I will make thy name (renowned) when thou hast reached the horizon, having passed by the battlements of Him-whose-name-is-Hidden. Strength comes forth from my flesh, power having assailed my flesh, power having attained its peak. When the Radiant One has journeyed, he has made his own seat, being seated at the head of the gods in the entourage of The Releaser (?).

O Falcon, my son Horus, dwell in this land of your father Osiris in this your name of Falcon who is on the battlements of the Mansion of Him-whose-name-is-Hidden. I ask that you may be in the following of Re-Akhty in the prow of the bark of the Primeval One for ever.

[STAGE DIRECTION]

Isis goes down to The Releaser (?) who brought Horus, for Isis had asked that he should be The Releaser (?) as leader of eternity.

[ISIS]

See ye Horus, O ye gods.

HORUS

I am Horus, the great Falcon who is on the battlements of Him-whose-name-is-Hidden. My flight has reached the horizon, I have passed the gods of the sky so that I have made my position superior to that of the Primeval Gods. The Contender (?) cannot attain my first flight. My place is far distant from that of Seth, the enemy of my father Osiris. I have conquered the ways of eternity at dawn, I am distinguished in my flight. There is no god who can do what I have done. I will attack the enemy of my father Osiris, he being placed under my sandals in this my name of Ademu. I am Horus born of Isis whose protection was made in the egg and (therefore) the fiery blast of your mouths cannot reach me. I am Horus, more exalted (lit. 'distant') of position than gods and men. I am Horus son of Isis.

I personally feel that this may well be part of a play, but it is impossible to prove and there are some real difficulties. The most important are concerned with the way in which some of the speakers are introduced. In a play, and according to Drioton's criteria, one would expect at the beginning of a speech the name only of the speaker or 'x says'. When however, this text uses such phrases as 'Ho, says Re-Atum, let your heart be wise', or 'Hear this ye gods, said Isis, which Atum . . . has said', the Egyptian words are used in a normal narrative style, not in the way expected in a play. This is a serious objection; the same occurs in some of the other fragments but Drioton does not appear to have appreciated the point. Nevertheless, this is a very interesting fragment. Particularly striking is the way in which the birth of Horus is presented through the actual words of Isis in her third speech.

All the texts of possible examples of Egyptian drama mentioned above are to a greater or lesser degree essentially religious. Drioton's examples are almost exclusively fragments removed from their original context and re-used for magical purposes. The others, such as the Ramesseum Papyrus and the Shabaka Stone, may best be termed ritual or liturgical dramas. This is not surprising, for drama seems to have grown and developed from liturgy, a process that can be seen clearly in early church ritual and mediaeval drama. It would only be natural for Egyptian drama to have developed in the same way. The writer is convinced that there was drama in Ancient Egypt but, until *The Triumph of Horus* was identified and studied, there was no hint that it had developed beyond liturgical drama. Here lies the interest and importance of *The Triumph of Horus:* if there was one play that was not purely ritual drama, could there not be others? Could there not be a secular drama?

Drioton, in fact, claimed that there was a secular drama in Egypt, performed by strolling players. His authority was a Middle Kingdom stela of a man named Emhab. As at the time he wrote the stela had not been published, Drioton was only able to print and translate a very few sentences: for most scholars it was therefore impossible to control the text and the context. The picture Drioton drew was of a man, Emhab, who followed his actor master wherever he went, and whose function was more or less to act as stooge. A fascinating picture. This view was contested by Vikentiev (see Bibliography) with vigour but not, it transpires, with absolute accuracy. Only recently has a photograph and hand copy of the stela become available. The edition of Professor J. Černý,[29] published shortly after his death, proves conclusively that Emhab was neither strolling player nor stooge, he was much more senior in rank, and his autobiographical text has no reference to drama.

2 *The Background of the Play*

POSITION OF THE PLAY ON THE TEMPLE WALL

The typical Egyptian temple is separated, and protected, from the outside world by a stout and high brick wall in which there is normally a monumental gateway more or less on the axis of the temple: there may on occasion be side entrances in this wall. Within the sacred enclosure or temenos thus formed were situated the principal temple, a sacred lake, sometimes subsidiary temples or chapels, and a number of buildings and storehouses. In the Pharaonic temples the temple itself does not appear always to have been clearly separated from the administrative buildings, though at Karnak the Middle Kingdom and Eighteenth Dynasty portions of the temple were in fact surrounded by a stone enclosure wall, which thus created a relatively narrow corridor round the main buildings.

The temples of the Graeco-Roman Period were slightly different. The first unit was itself a complete temple with hypostyle hall, one or more additional halls, the sanctuary and a number of side rooms or chapels. To this original nucleus was added an outer hypostyle or pronaos which was both wider and loftier than the rest of the temple. Beyond the pronaos was the peristyle forecourt and the pylons. A great stone wall was built from the pylons and surrounded the whole temple. This wall thus formed the side walls of the forecourt and created a corridor, called by the Egyptians the Pure Ambulatory, between it and the main fabric of the temple (fig. 4, p. 45). The scenes of *The Triumph of Horus* are engraved on the inner (east) face of the west enclosure wall.

The decoration of this great stone enclosure wall is distributed over three registers, the lowest register being regarded as the first. The decoration of a temple is always orderly, there is always a logical development and the normal rule is that the order of the scenes is from the entrance of the temple to the rear. The Temple of Edfu faces south, its main axis being south to north, and in each unit the decoration of the walls to left and right of the axis is normally to be read from south to north; in those rooms that are at right angles to the axis the decoration develops from the door of the room to the middle line of the rear wall. For special reasons, which need not concern us here, there are a few exceptions to this rule but the normal order is from south to north.

The decoration of the inner face of the west enclosure wall departs from this basic rule. In the first register there are 15 great scenes and in the second register there are 16, the unequal distribution of the scenes being due to the fact that the extreme south end of the first register is really the narrow passage between the enclosure wall and the pronaos that links the ambulatory with the forecourt. In the following pages these individual scenes are called 'Reliefs' with appropriate serial number in order to distinguish them from the 'Scenes' in the various Acts of the play. Thus Relief 4 in the first register is Act I, Scene i of the play.

The first register begins in the normal way at the extreme south end with Reliefs 1 and 2 but the following 11 reliefs have to be read in the opposite order from north to south, Relief 13 thus being engraved on the wall immediately after Relief 2. Thereafter Reliefs 14 and 15 are to be read in the usual way from south to north. Reliefs 3 to 13 give the text and reliefs of our play *The Triumph of Horus* (fig. 1). Similarly,

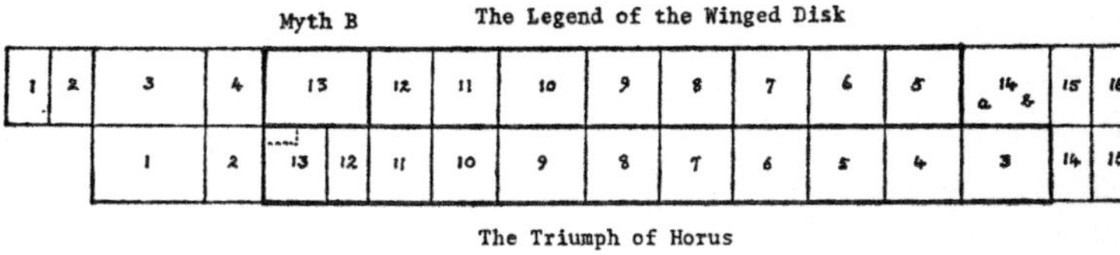

		Myth B			The Legend of the Winged Disk										
1	2	3	4	15	12	11	10	9	8	7	6	5	14 a & b	15	16
		1	2	13	12	11	10	9	8	7	6	5	4	3	14	15

The Triumph of Horus

FIGURE I   Edfu: Arrangement of the reliefs on the west enclosure wall (first two registers)

in the second register Reliefs 1 to 4 are read from south to north but the next Reliefs, 5 to 13, read from north to south and the last three reliefs on the wall, Reliefs 14 to 16, are once more in the usual order from south to north.

The unusual arrangement of the reliefs in these two registers is clear evidence of a deliberate intention to isolate the reliefs read in the reverse order from the remaining reliefs on the wall and to indicate that in each register they formed a unit. These texts and reliefs in fact form part of what is called the Myth of Horus which is preserved at Edfu in five main texts[1]. Text A, Reliefs 5 to 12 in the second register, is the Legend of the Winged Disk,[2] an aetiological narrative, given a spurious authenticity by being dated to regnal year 363 of Re-Harakhte, of the fights up and down Egypt between Horus and his followers and

Seth and his followers, together with punning explanations of the names assigned to places and persons mentioned in the narrative: it is in fact a combination of propaganda to justify the pre-eminence of Horus the Behdetite and a potent spell to protect the King of Egypt on the day of combat. Myth B, Relief 13 in register two, is a short text very similar to the Legend of the Winged Disk but nevertheless not a part of it. Myth C, in register one, Reliefs 3 to 13, is *The Triumph of Horus*. The latter certainly formed part of the Festival of Victory (see below p. 27), and it is a reasonable assumption that Texts A and B were also parts of the same festival.

It has also been claimed (see below p. 25) that Relief 14 in the second register should, too, be included in these groups of reliefs to be read from north to south but that its correct place in the ritual is after Relief 13 in the first register. Relief 14 is really two ritual episodes combined in what at first sight might seem to be a single relief; it is a not uncommon device of the Egyptian artist to combine two or more episodes, which may be separated in time and space, into an outwardly single, unitary composition. Relief 14 is connected with the Festival of Sokaris, which was celebrated annually at Edfu almost exactly two months earlier than the Festival of Victory: there is no logical or reasonable possibility of its being connected with the scenes that concern us.

The Triumph of Horus is therefore to be found in Reliefs 3 to 13 in the first register. Relief 3 is the Prologue; Reliefs 4 to 8 are the five scenes of Act I; Reliefs 9 and 10 are the two scenes of Act II; Reliefs 11 to 13 are the three scenes of Act III; the dotted rectangle in the top left hand corner of Relief 13 marks the position of the Epilogue, which has no relief of its own.

The decoration of the inner face of the west enclosure wall of Edfu was completed in the reigns of Ptolemy IX, Soter II and his younger brother Ptolemy X, Alexander I. The history of this period of the Ptolemaic Dynasty is very complicated, largely owing to the ruthless and dominating personality of Cleopatra III, mother of both kings, and her violent personal prejudices. A very brief outline of events is essential in order to establish the approximate date of the engraving of *The Triumph of Horus* on the wall. Ptolemy IX was the eldest son of Ptolemy VIII, Euergetes II and Cleopatra III. He came to the throne in 116 B.C. as joint ruler with his mother, apparently much against her will, for she appears to have preferred her younger son. In 110 Cleopatra III forced him to accept Ptolemy X as joint ruler but only for a very short time. In 108 there was another short joint reign of the two brothers which ended in civil war and the expulsion of Ptolemy IX, who lived in exile until 88. Ptolemy x in the meantime ruled with Cleopatra iii until her death in 101, thereafter he reigned with his wife Cleopatra Berenice, daughter of Ptolemy ix. In 88 Ptolemy ix reconquered Egypt and drove out Ptolemy x, who died in a fight at sea. Ptolemy ix then reigned with Cleopatra Berenice until his death in 81. Cleopatra Berenice then reigned alone for a short time but married in 80 her step-son Ptolemy xi, Alexander ii, who murdered her 19 days after their marriage and who in turn was murdered by the enraged Alexandrians.

These political events are reflected in the names of the kings. There is a slight difference in the cartouche names of Ptolemy ix before and after his exile. In the first register Reliefs 3 to 15, and in the second register Reliefs 5 to 16 the cartouches, though not completely engraved, are those of the first reign of Ptolemy ix, and in both registers the only queen mentioned is Cleopatra iii. Since Cleopatra died in 101 and since the cartouches of Ptolemy x are completely different from those of Ptolemy ix and at Edfu always include his name Alexander, it is evident that all the inscriptions of Myths A, B and C must have been completed before the flight of Ptolemy ix in 107. The exact year of the completion is unknown but since Relief 3 on the second register bears the name of Ptolemy x, Alexander i, it is reasonable to assume that the engraving of the texts of the Myth of Horus was completed towards the end of the first reign of Ptolemy ix. As a rough working hypothesis it may be suggested that the engraving of *The Triumph of Horus* was completed by approximately 110 B.C. It is evident that the texts and reliefs of the Myth of Horus were completed as a unit before proceeding to engrave the scenes on both registers that are to the left (south) of them and before even beginning the decoration of the third register.

THE TEXTS AND RELIEFS

The composition of the 11 reliefs that form *The Triumph of Horus* may easily be seen by study of Plate 1, a photograph of Act ii, Scene i, and of the line drawings (figs. 6–16) of each scene in the play which are reproduced at the head of each scene. In all but Relief 12 (Act iii, Scene ii) the relief is on the right of the beholder and to its left is a long hieroglyphic text in vertical columns which fill the whole height of the register. With the exception of Relief 11 (Act iii, Scene i) there is a long horizontal line of text over the figures.

Reliefs 4–8 are the successive scenes of Act i. In each are depicted two boats, reproductions in wood of the papyrus canoes in which, in early times, hippopotami were hunted in the marshes. In each boat Horus, accompanied by a demon with the head of an ape, a bull or a lion, stabs a hippopotamus with his harpoon. Relief 9 (Act II, Scene i) is dominated by the war-galley of Horus in full sail and clearly depicts action on land and water. The following relief (Act II, Scene ii) also indicates actors on land and water but the boat again is different: it is a simplified form of the state barge of Horus in which the victorious god is to receive the insignia of kingship and to be crowned. The last three reliefs (11 to 13) are those of the scenes of Act III: no boats are depicted, for the whole of this Act, naturally, was performed on land.

The long vertical columns contain the main text of the play. It will at once be noticed that the individual speeches are not clearly separated. In fact, the speakers very often are not indicated, though occasionally a speaker is explicitly named. The identity of most of the speakers has to be deduced from the internal evidence of the text. There are certain inherent dangers in this and on occasion an identification can be disputed. Nevertheless, close and detailed study of the text has made possible the attribution of words to speakers, even when unnamed, with confidence and a very high degree of certainty.

In the reliefs themselves the identity of the individual figures is assured because the short columns of hieroglyphs above them give their names and epithets and titles, while a vertical column in front of each figure gives the words of the speech to be uttered by each person. With a single exception (fig. 14: Act III, Scene i) there is a horizontal line of text over each relief (but not extending over the long vertical columns of hieroglyphs) which is not immediately and obviously linked with any of the figures in the reliefs (see below p. 39).

The decoration of a temple wall, the choice and arrangement of the scenes engraved upon it, is deliberate and purposeful; each scene is in the only place suited to it in the particular ritual of which it forms part, and each scene fits into a rigid order of succession which is not, and cannot be, broken. Each scene or relief and its accompanying texts is a complete entity in itself, separate from the other reliefs before or after it on the walls. The only exception to this rule is formed by those few instances in which, according to a well-established principle of Egyptian art, what at first is a single composition in reality contains two or more separate episodes or actions; even in these, each scene is complete in itself within the frame of the relief and does not, and cannot, over-flow into an adjacent relief. It therefore follows that each of the 11 great reliefs that form *The Triumph of Horus* is complete in itself, and that the actual reliefs and the long vertical columns of text form parts of one and the same episode.

It is obvious, however, that in preparing a complete text of the play the question of how to combine the evidence of the reliefs and the texts presents a very real problem. It is made all the more difficult because they do not mechanically duplicate each other. Characters depicted in the reliefs do not occur in the long texts, and vice-versa. Why this should be so and how reliefs and texts are to be combined will be discussed more fully later in this chapter (pp. 36–45).

IS THE TRIUMPH OF HORUS A PLAY?

It is the main thesis of this book that *The Triumph of Horus* is a play, a somewhat primitive religious drama acted annually at Edfu during the Festival of Victory. In form it is a play and falls easily and automatically into acts and scenes without any manipulation of the reliefs or their order. The acts are distinct from each other in their content, yet they show a consistent development of the main theme. In the text we find many explicit references to individual speakers, a limited number of stage directions which would be difficult to explain except as parts of a drama, even a little elementary characterisation. It is certainly 'dramatic', it even has a certain degree of tension and excitement, and it is obviously designed to give an important part to a Chorus and to cater for a strong element of audience participation. We cannot, of course, know whether the whole play has been preserved: the strict limits imposed by the available space on the temple wall may very well have caused the abbreviation of speeches and songs, or even the complete elimination of some of them and of some characters, but what remains at Edfu is a complete play, possibly abbreviated but still a play. It would be very surprising if such a play, derived as it is from more than one very ancient myth, had not undergone considerable editing. It would be equally surprising if such editing and attempts to unite and reconcile different myths should not, in view of the invincible conservatism of the Egyptians, have resulted at times in contradictions and inconsistencies; they are common in Egyptian religious texts. Granted all this, the play still remains a play.

It must be pointed out, however, that this view of the text has not won universal acceptance. Both the late Canon Etienne Drioton and the late Maurice Alliot have published studies of the Edfu text in which they firmly deny that it represents a play, though they admit the existence of certain 'dramatic' elements. This is not the place for controversy or detailed criticism of these views, which are not in agreement with each other, but it would be wrong to pass them over in silence.

Drioton did not mention *The Triumph of Horus* in his *Le Théâtre égyptien* though its dramatic nature had been summarily mentioned in 1935.[3] In 1948, however, he published almost simultaneously a popular article in Cairo[4] and a book[5] with detailed commentary in which he attacked the very idea that the text as it exists at Edfu is that of a play. In his opinion the Edfu texts contain an edited and reorganised version of two earlier plays. These earlier plays he calls Text A and Text B. Text A, according to him, is the text of the war-galley (which may be roughly vocalised *ahat*), with action on the river bank and with Busiris as the place of origin or inspiration. Text B is the text of the skiff or canoe (*depet*), Buto is the place associated with it and the action is on the water. Text A is the story of the fights between Horus, a strong, mature man, and Seth and his associates as hippopotami; Text B depicts the immature youth fighting against the Monster. Armed with these criteria, Drioton dissected the text, but not the texts accompanying the reliefs, into sections, often very small, which were then reassembled in a quite different order. In the process some sentences in the long vertical columns of hieroglyphs no longer appear in Texts A and B. The reliefs and their texts are completely ignored.

The result of these extremely ingenious efforts is two short playlets with severely restricted speaking parts. Text A consists of a Prologue, in which Thoth congratulates Horus. Four scenes then follow: Scene 1, The Preparation of Horus; Scene 2, The Spear of Onuris; Scene 3, The Departure of the War-galley; Scene 4, The Triumphant Return. Finally there is an Epilogue, The Dismemberment of the Hippopotamus.

Text B also begins with a Prologue, The Advice of Isis. It continues with six scenes: Scene 1, Arming for the Fight; Scene 2, The Approach of the Monster; Scene 3, The Intervention of Isis; Scene 4, Isis Encourages her Son; Scene 5, The *coup de grâce*; Scene 6, The Triumphant Return. Finally, an Epilogue, The Dismemberment of the Hippopotamus, followed by a brief monologue describing the results of the victory—a new city built in Buto, a glorious reign of Horus, and the moral is drawn that it is good for a son to succeed his father and vindicate him, and that he should give thanks to god.

Having explained to his own satisfaction the original form of the texts, it was still necessary to explain what is actually on the temple wall. Drioton's explanation is that the 11 great scenes are part of the liturgy of harpooning the hippopotamus and that the texts are hymns sung at appropriate moments in the ritual. He divides these hymns into two main groups: psalms (*psaumes*) and songs (*cantiques*), which are read for the most part consecutively from Relief 3 to Relief 13, though there is still some upsetting of individual words and texts. The words 'Hold fast, Horus, hold fast' serve as convenient termination of most of the 'psalms'. In this way Drioton obtained, after an introductory song, ten psalms, each representing one of the ten harpoons; seven further psalms covering most of Acts II and III; then Conclusion (equivalent to the dismemberment of the hippopotamus in Act III, Scene iii, plus the Epilogue), then a Finale, taken from Act III, Scene iii (III. iii. 1–8), a Rubric (equals III.iii.9–10; 13–15) and a Supplement consisting of Psalm XVIII (equals III.iii.42–54) and Psalm XIX (equals III.iii.55–80). These psalms, however, do not quite exhaust all the texts, and after all there are a few nice pieces in the reliefs. Hence the whole series is ended by the 'songs' (*cantiques*) of Edfu. The first, entitled 'The Triumphant Procession' is an amalgam of III.ii.15–21 plus III.ii.1–9 plus III.iii.43–54 plus II.ii.1–11 (it is not clear why III.iii.43–54 had to be repeated here and in Psalm XVIII). The second, 'The Choirs of Women', is composed of II.ii.36–51, but not arranged antiphonically as in our translation. The third song 'The Song of the Harpooners', is based on II.i.1–11. Apart from the extracts included in the 'songs', the evidence of the reliefs is totally disregarded.

These various reconstructions are brilliant and ingenious examples of mental gymnastics but the chances of their being correct are minimal. The disregard of the reliefs is a serious error: it has to be insisted once more that texts and reliefs cannot be divorced and his neglect to pay due heed to the reliefs has deprived Drioton of the vital clue to the true meaning of the whole. The justification for the identification of Texts A and B is extremely slender. 'War-galley' occurs seven times (Prologue 32.45; I.i.25.40; I.iii.74; II.i.3; III.i.16). The word 'skiff' (*depet*) is even more infrequent; it occurs only twice in identical passages 'The boat is light and he who is in it is a child' (I.iii.27; I.iv.48). In five of the 11 scenes of the play neither word occurs at all; surely a very fragile foundation for such radical regroupings and reconstitutions of the text.

A detailed discussion of Drioton's views and theories would be completely out of place here and will not be attempted. But it must be pointed out that the importance of his key words is in reality very doubtful. *Depet*, for instance, is the normal Egyptian word for 'boat'; Drioton has assigned to it the meaning 'skiff', solely on the basis of 'the boat is light', but the word 'light' is identical in spelling with the word 'aged' and it is impossible to decide whether the correct translation is not 'the boat is aged and he who is in it is a child'.

The war-galley also has far less significance than Drioton claims. It was his view that each of the sections of his Text A were introduced by a special key-phrase. This introductory phrase for his Text A, Scene 3, is borrowed from I.i.39–40, 'Goodly Falcon who boards his boat and takes to the river in his war-galley'. Drioton translates this 'He is the Goodly Falcon who has boarded his boat when he takes to the river in his war-galley'; this translation is only possible if the text is emended and a word inserted which does not occur in any of the parallels. The word translated here as 'boat' is written in the text of the play by a simple ideogram and is not spelled out; the passage occurs elsewhere in Edfu texts and in two instances[6] is spelled out fully and proves to be *depet*! Drioton's criterion, therefore, is non-existent. The real interest and importance of the war-galley is not its function as a fictitious indicator of a lost play but its symbolism. In the texts of the play, and in numerous other Edfu texts, it is clear that the war-galley is Isis holding, guarding and nursing her son. This symbolism is made very clear; it is, of course, entirely contrary to the view put forward by Drioton.

The cities of Buto and Busiris similarly do not have the significance that is supposed to be attached to them. Buto, in one of its forms Pe and Dep, Dep or Djebawet occurs six times; Busiris is also mentioned five times. Both places are mentioned in the list of towns and cities in I.iii.45.46, and in the dismemberments of the hippopotamus in III.i.9 and III.iii.43.89.96.98): they are obviously no more significant than the other places mentioned. Again in III.iii we find 'Be glad, ye women of Busiris' (III.iii.43) and 'Rejoice, ye women of Wetjeset-Hor' (III.iii.45); in these passages Busiris and Wetjeset-Hor are obviously in parallel, with no other function but to express the dichotomy Lower Egypt and Upper Egypt.

On the other hand the references to Buto and Busiris in II.ii are interesting and important. The phrase 'The Lower Egyptian Princesses and the women of Busiris' (II.ii.36–7) is logical but the parallel 'The Upper Egyptian Princesses and the women of Pe and Dep' (II.ii.40–1) is manifestly wrong; instead of Pe and Dep (Buto) one would have expected the name of some Upper Egyptian city, in all probability Wetjeset-Hor. The most likely explanation is that at this point the priestly scribe used and adapted, very carelessly and clumsily, a Lower Egyptian prototype, but it would be unwise and unjustified to press the point further.

Drioton is entirely correct in seeing a Lower Egyptian element in the play. As we shall see later, Act I is a harpoon ritual and is beyond doubt an adaptation of a very ancient royal harpooning ritual of Lower Egyptian origin. In a play such as *The Triumph of Horus*, which is essentially a drama of kingship in which two main myths had to be combined and adapted to express the Egyptian concept of kingship, and in which also the dual nature of Egypt had to be expressed in terms of the King of Upper Egypt and the King of Lower Egypt, it was inevitable and essential for strong Lower Egyptian elements to be present. Moreover, it is a characteristic feature of many of the major Edfu texts that a marked Memphite and Lower Egyptian influence can be seen. The Egyptians themselves were well aware of this; in one text at Edfu it is even stated that Edfu and Upper Egypt were colonised from the North. Though much research will be needed before the precise implications of the Lower Egyptian elements are fully understood, the fact that they exist neither justifies nor proves the extreme thesis advanced by Drioton.

The second study of *The Triumph of Horus* was that of the late Maurice Alliot. In 1944 Alliot completed the manuscript of his monumental study *Le Culte d'Horus à Edfou au temps des Ptolémées*. It was not until after the War that he became aware of the work of Drioton on drama in Ancient Egypt or of the English translation and commentary on *The Triumph of Horus*. Only then did his completed manuscript reach Cairo and it was not until 1954 that his work was published in two volumes, his study of the Myth of Horus forming Volume II, pp. 677–822. By the time his book appeared in print Alliot had naturally been able to study the divergent views of Drioton and Blackman and Fairman. As far as can be judged without having seen the original manuscript, his main thesis and interpretations were unchanged, though he introduced a few relatively minor changes in translation.

Alliot denied that *The Triumph of Horus* was a drama, though he admitted the 'dramatic' flavour of some sections of the text. His view was based on two assumptions. The first was that Registers One and Two are not independent but form a unit in which is found a ritual performed at the annual Festival of Victory. The second assumption was that the original intention of the decorators of the temple was that the scenes of *The Triumph of Horus* and the Legend of the Winged Disk should fill exactly the same relative space but owing to an error on the part of the sculptors the scenes on the lower register were allowed to occupy too much space. In order to correct this presumed error, the nine reliefs of the Legend of the Winged Disk (fig. 1: Register Two,

Reliefs 5 to 12) were centred over Reliefs 4 to 11 in the first register. In order to fill the spaces at either end of The Legend of the Winged Disk, Relief 14 (fig. 1: Register Two) was added at the north end, though according to Alliot it was the final act of the whole ritual and should logically have been placed after (to the left, south) of Relief 13 in the first register, and similarly Relief 13 (actually Myth B) was placed after Relief 12 (fig. 1: Register Two). But, according to Alliot, the object of this hypothetical operation was that the scenes of the ritual should be equally distributed over both registers to form a neat rectangle, Relief 13 ought to have formed part of the ritual: this Alliot did not admit; he did not include Relief 13 (Myth B) in his reconstruction of the ritual, he did not even attempt to translate it. On these grounds alone his theory of the decoration of the wall breaks down. All our experience shows that the decoration of the temple walls was planned and executed with extreme care and accuracy in advance of any attempt to begin the actual engraving; at Edfu in particular every wall was planned and every scene was positioned with meticulous care, and the chances of errors being committed after the decoration had actually been commenced can be excluded. If the scenes in the two registers are unequal in extent, we may be confident that such was the intention of the decorator.

There was, however, a third assumption on which Alliot based his reconstruction. Reliefs 5 to 12 of the Second Register were, he claimed, a narrative of the wars of Horus and Seth which preceded and was in parallel with Reliefs 4 to 8 of the First Register (the whole of our Act I), which were the ritual enactment of the narrative portion. Thus he linked successively two of the places in which fighting occurred in the narrative with two of the harpoons in the successive scenes of Act I. For example, his first episode is composed of Register Two, Reliefs 5, 6 and part only of 7, followed by Register One, Relief 5 (our Act I, Scene i). This is entirely contrary to rule: this zigzagging from register to register within a single ritual episode is impossible. Moreover, the supposed parallelism between the places mentioned in the narrative in Register Two and the harpoons in Register One is non-existent: for example, the first two combats are said to take place at Edfu (in reality there were two separate fights at different places in the neighbourhood of Edfu but Alliot conveniently ignores this fact) and at another otherwise unknown place called Djedem, approximately 13 miles south-east of Thebes. The combats in these two places are equated by Alliot with the first two harpoons (our Act I, Scene i). But as we shall see (p. 39 below) the ten harpoons of Act I are grouped in pairs, of which the odd numbers (Harpoons 1, 3, 5, 7 and 9) represent Lower Egypt and are wielded by Horus Lord of Mesen, and the even numbered (Harpoons 2, 4, 6, 8 and 10) represent Upper Egypt and are wielded by Horus the Behdetite. If Alliot's thesis were correct, the town in parallel with the first harpoon would have to be in the Delta and could not be Edfu. There is thus no correlation, geographical or other, between the texts of the two registers and the whole of Alliot's thesis and interpretation collapses.

A very brief summary of Alliot's reconstruction gives the following scheme:

A Introduction (Register One, Relief 3 = our Prologue).
B Part I: The Ritual of the Ten Harpoons.
   (*a*) The ritual is divided into five sections each composed of one or more of the Reliefs 5 to 11 of the Second Register plus one of the Reliefs 4 to 8 of the First Register (according to our theory Act I, Scenes i to v).
   (*b*) A text composed of Register Two, Relief 11, lines 5 (end) to 11 and Relief 12, lines 1–2 (half). This, according to Alliot, does not form part of the ritual. The remaining 9½ lines of Relief 12 are not translated and are not included in the reconstruction.
C Part II. This section (Register One, Reliefs 9 and 10) is said to be an interval; the action of the ceremony stops and there is an interlude of song and dance (our Act II, Scene i and ii). Alliot regards this section as essentially a summary of the fight and the celebration of the victory.
D Part III. The Sacrifice of the Hippopotamus, divided into three sections (Register One, Reliefs 11, 12, 13), which correspond to our Act III, Scenes i, ii and iii. Alliot omits the Epilogue.
E Part IV: Concluding Rites (Register Two, Relief 14). This, Alliot claims, is the concluding rite of the whole ceremony of the Festival of Victory: it acts as the presentation of food, which he claims must be the final episode of every ritual and symbolises the renewal of the strength of Harakhte, the conqueror of Seth. The scene, which at first sight looks like a single composition, in reality represents two acts: on the left (fig. 1: Register Two, Relief 14a) is the offering of Incense; on the right (fig. 1: Register Two, Relief 14b) is the Dragging of Sokaris. The latter ceremony is very well known: it marks the dragging of Sokaris on a sledge around the temple and was celebrated 'on the sacred morning' on the Fourth Month of the Inundation Season, day 26, almost exactly two months before the Festival of Victory.

It would be pointless, here, to devote further space to this reconstruction. We have summarised Alliot's views as fairly as possible but there is no possibility of their being correct.

The fact that the divergent views of both Alliot and Drioton cannot be accepted does not, of course, automatically imply that *The Triumph of Horus* is a play. The fact that the full text as printed below looks and reads like a play and as such convinced those responsible for the production at Padgate (see Chapter 3) is not in itself proof that the Egyptian original was a play. It is the basic argument of this book that the reliefs and the text form a whole and that only by combining the two can the real play be recovered. Nevertheless, the printed text is a reconstruction, in a form that has never been presented in the previous studies. The reader, therefore, may fairly and justifiably ask: what confidence can one place on this version? is it not merely the product of yet another modern imagination—and equally fictitious?

The editor concerned with translating and reconstructing such a text is faced with a very heavy burden of responsibility, for it is very easy to project purely modern, contemporary ideas, even prejudices, and produce a work of pure fiction. The text, its composition, the principles and rules on which the play has been reconstructed and set out are explained in greater detail below (pp. 36–45). For the present it is sufficient simply to state the essential facts. To the objective student of the original the division of the text into three major divisions (which we call 'Acts') and each division into a number of sub-sections (which we call 'Scenes') is inescapable and obligatory. It will be noticed that Alliot, though he uses a different terminology, uses an identical division of the component elements: he recognises the Prologue but he omits, of course, the Epilogue and adds the Dragging of Sokaris. The external shape and form of the work is obvious and certain. Even if the reliefs be disregarded, the main texts in the long vertical columns undeniably are those of a drama. They contain three very good indicators of a play: first, in many places the names of the actors are placed before the words they have to speak; second, the whole text is a series of speeches and songs, without any narrative; third, the presence of indubitable stage directions which in grammatical form and in content differ from the rest of the text. The whole text is clearly a conscious composition, each Act complete in itself but with a real development from Act to Act and a consistent theme from Prologue to Epilogue. It contains a strong element of that conflict, in the wider sense of the word and not just physical combat, that is such an important element of most drama. It even shows, though this is not an essential, some elementary characterisation, above all in the character of Isis. There are strong indications that the text enshrines a genuine drama. It is a primitive type of drama; it is more properly a ritual drama in the sense of a play about ritual but not a ritual composed and designed for a particular purpose and a particular occasion—note how Greek tragedy could only, in origin, be performed on a particular date or occasion.

STORY AND SIGNIFICANCE OF THE PLAY

The play was acted annually at Edfu on the twenty-first day of the second month of Winter and on each of the following four days. Ideally these five days were equivalent to 9–13 January, but in 110 B.C., the approximate date of the engraving of the text on the walls of the temple, the date would have been 9–13 March. The reason for this apparent discrepancy is to be found in the nature of the Egyptian calendar. The Egyptian year was of 365 days, divided into three seasons, Inundation, Winter and Summer. Each season consisted of four months, each of 30 days. Five additional days, the so-called epagomenal days, completed the year. New Year's Day, the first day of the first month of Inundation, was traditionally the first day of the annual rise of the Nile; it also was the day of the heliacal rising of Sothis, the Dog-star Sirius, 19 July (Julian). Each year, therefore, there was a difference of approximately a quarter of a day between the Egyptian calendar year and the true year, one day in every four years. The Egyptians did not attempt to correct this by a leap year or some other device but allowed the error to accumulate until, after a cycle of approximately 1456 years, the years were once more in accord and the process began all over again.

The play formed part of the annual Festival of Victory and commemorated the wars between Horus and Seth, the victory of Horus and his coronation as king of a united Egypt, the dismemberment of the body of his defeated enemy, and his final triumph or justification.

The story is very simple. The Prologue has as its main object praise of the King and the happy days of festival and triumph, and the anticipatory declaration of the results of the whole play, the defeat of Seth and the triumph of Horus and the King. The five scenes of Act I embody somewhat formally, and in a combination of mime and drama, the ancient Harpoon Ritual: in each scene two forms of Horus, representing Lower and Upper Egypt, each thrust a harpoon into the body of a hippopotamus, which represents the Seth, the enemy of Horus. The significance of ten harpoons in all is unknown. Thus in Act I we find the formalised re-enactment of the way in which Horus defeated his enemy. Scene iv in this Act is interrupted by a brief interlude in which another ancient ritual—the killing of multi-coloured snakes (*sabet*-snakes, probably cobras) in Letopolis—is mimed: in dumb show the snakes are killed, their flesh eaten and their blood swallowed, the whole representing the destruction of the enemy. Act II is concerned primarily with the rejoicings over the victory achieved in the first act. In Scene i Isis, still apparently carried away by excitement, though Seth is already defeated, continues to incite her son's supporters and recites a very fine poem to the war-galley of Horus. In Scene ii Horus, having first mimed on land the killing of the hippopotamus, embarks on his ceremonial bark, is invested with the insignia of kingship and crowned as King of Upper and Lower Egypt and a double chorus, representing the women of Upper and Lower Egypt, sing antiphonically a hymn of rejoicing over the victory. In Act III are the final celebrations, two versions of the dismemberment of the hippopotamus, the severed portions of the body being distributed among the gods, and the triumph of Horus, the gods and the King is proclaimed. The play ends with a brief Epilogue in which the Reader formally declares that Horus, certain divinities and places and lastly the King himself are triumphant over their enemies.

Superficially, therefore, the play is the enactment of a mythological situation, the wars between two gods, Horus and Seth. These wars, it should be noted, rest ultimately on a historical basis. In reality, however, the theme and purpose of the play are more complex and subtle.

The theme of the play is really Kingship, especially the renewal of the victorious power of the reigning king. In order the better to understand this it is necessary to know a little about Horus. The mythology of Horus is extremely complicated, there are many forms of Horus, though of course not all were of equal importance, and many myths associated with him. For our immediate purpose, however, only two aspects need be mentioned, in very abbreviated and simplified form.

The first theme is that of two brothers, Horus and Seth, who fought each other for the mastery and rule of Egypt. This is the earliest element and undoubtedly goes back to prehistoric, predynastic times, i.e. to before 3000 B.C. Originally, it seems, Horus was the god of Lower Egypt and Seth the god of Upper Egypt, but Horus conquered and colonised Upper Egypt. Hence the roles of Horus and Seth came to be reversed. When hostilities were resumed, it was the Horus clans of Upper Egypt who eventually defeated the clans of Lower Egypt, the Delta, Mythologically this was the victory of Horus over Seth; historically it was the Union of the Two Lands and the foundation of the First Dynasty under the leadership of the Horus-kings of Upper Egypt. As long as pharaonic civilisation lasted, long after the dawn of the Christian Era, this dual nature of Egypt was never forgotten. This idea was expressed in two of the five official names of every king, in the 'Two Mistresses' name (the Two Mistresses being the Vulture-goddess of Upper Egypt and the Uraeus-goddess of Lower Egypt) and in the name as 'King of Upper and Lower Egypt'; it was expressed in the very common royal title 'Lord of the Two Lands'; it was even reflected in the administration, particularly in the Old Kingdom, where the treasury is the 'Double Treasury' (literally, the 'Two Houses of Silver') and the royal granary is the 'Double Granary'. As a further consequence, in theory every royal ritual had to be a double one, each episode being performed once for Upper Egypt and once for Lower Egypt. This last fact has an immediate and important bearing on the reconstruction and significance of *The Triumph of Horus*.

The second element in the mythology of Horus to which reference must be made is that of the Osiris Cycle: this is a later development. According to this legend Osiris was a good and beneficent king who was murdered by his brother Seth. Horus, the posthumous son of Osiris, was reared and hidden by his mother Isis in the marshes of the Delta, on the mythical island of Khemmis near Buto. When Horus had grown up he fought against his uncle Seth to avenge his father and to recover his inheritance, the kingship of Egypt. One aspect of the conflict between Horus and Seth was a law-suit before a tribunal of the gods themselves. According to one story, recorded in a papyrus of the New Kingdom, this law-suit lasted 80 years and resulted in the tribunal's verdict that Horus was the legitimate son of Osiris and legitimate successor to his throne.

Inevitably these two originally separate elements became almost inextricably confused. Both are expressed repeatedly from beginning to end of *The Triumph of Horus*. Their joint result was that in Egypt Horus was the royal god. Every King of Egypt was Horus, the living Horus upon earth, because those Upper Egyptian kings who defeated Lower Egypt and founded the First Dynasty were worshippers of Horus. Hence from the beginning of the First Dynasty the first of the five official names of every king was his Horus-name. But Horus was also the son of Osiris, the dead, murdered king; he was thus legitimate king by primogeniture, by victory over Seth, by verdict of a divine tribunal and by virtue of having buried his father. Thus every Egyptian king was Horus and as such was legitimate ruler of Egypt.

The kingship, the divine kingship, was the central, dominant and enduring element in Egyptian life and society, the golden thread. It was this theory of a divine kingship, stretching unbroken from the living Horus-king to the first king of the First Dynasty, and beyond him through the dynasties of gods to the first god-king, the sun-god Re in person, that gave Egyptian civilisation its extraordinary stability, that gave the Egyptians a comfortable feeling that all was well and made even foreign rule and domination at least tolerable—just as long as the fiction of the unbroken thread was outwardly preserved.

It is in the light of these Egyptian views about kingship that the reliefs that accompany and illustrate the individual scenes of the play have their importance and significance. Indeed, without due consideration of the evidence of the reliefs the main hieroglyphic text is deprived of much of its meaning and the vital clue to the true purpose of the play is lost. Whoever reads only the text of the play will be puzzled by the duality present in the play. Why, for instance, in Act I are there *two* harpoons in each scene? Why, in Act III, are there *two* dismemberments? If, however, one studies the drawings of the individual scenes which are printed at the head of the translation, it will be noted that in each scene of Act I Horus is depicted twice (figs. 7–11). The texts that accompany these reliefs show clearly that these were not identical forms of Horus: in each scene the first harpoon is wielded by Horus Lord of Mesen and the second by Horus the Behdetite (fig. 3, p. 38), who represents respectively Lower Egypt and Upper Egypt. Here we have a graphic display of the fundamental fact that in every ritual concerned with kingship every rite or episode, because of the symbolism of the Two Lands (see p. 29 above), had to be performed twice, first for Lower Egypt and then for Upper Egypt, protocol demanding that Upper Egypt as the senior partner and conqueror of Lower Egypt should come last. Here is one of the proofs that the central theme of the play is kingship. It is largely because Alliot and Drioton did not pay due consideration to the reliefs that they failed to detect the true meaning of the play.

Scrutiny of the reliefs will reveal that it is only in Act I that two forms of Horus are depicted; in Acts II and III we never find more than one Horus, who is Horus the Behdetite. The reason for this is that the automatic consequence of the defeat of Seth in Act I is that henceforward there is only one king ruling over a united Egypt. This is clearly expressed when Horus is crowned with the Double Diadem and declares

> I take possession of the Two Lands
> In assuming the Double Diadem (II.ii.26–7)

The coronation in Act II, Scene ii, it should be noted, is very much abbreviated. In reality the imposition of the crowns in the elaborate ceremonial of the coronation consists of three main acts; first the imposition of the Red Crown of Lower Egypt, second the imposition of the White Crown of Upper Egypt, and finally the imposition of the Double Diadem (the red and white crowns united). It is impossible to determine with certainty whether it was deliberately intended that only an abbreviated version of the imposition of the crowns should be acted or whether lack of space dictated the omission of all but the crowning with the Double Diadem. It seems likely that the latter is the more probable explanation and that at the actual performance at Edfu all three impositions of crowns were enacted. This is the more probable for it is evident that the remainder of Act II, Scene ii is concerned with other episodes of the coronation ceremony. An extract from the coronation ritual is preserved on the third register of the same wall as that on which the play was engraved.[7] In this extract the imposition of the crowns is followed by three final episodes: acclamation of the newly crowned king; adoration of the king seated on his throne; and the bringing of offerings, symbolising the great banquet which was the final episode of the whole coronation ceremony. The acclamation and adoration of the king are undoubtedly represented in our play by the songs of the princesses and women of Upper and Lower Egypt and the final speeches of the scene. The banquet is not included in this scene; if it was desired to enact the banquet, it is conceivable that the dismemberment of the hippopotamus in Act III was imagined as representing it, though this cannot be stated with certainty. The dismemberment of the hippopotamus and the distribution of portions of its body did not merely demonstrate that the enemy was defeated and dead; it ensured, by the eating of his flesh, the absorption of his peculiar powers.

It might be objected that the relief of Act II, Scene ii (fig. 13, p. 105) contradicts the statement that only one form of Horus appears after the end of Act I because two figures of Horus are clearly to be seen in this scene. This, however, is not really so. Each Horus is clearly stated to be 'Horus the Behdetite, great god, lord of the sky, lord of Mesen' (II.ii.13) as though this single figure incorporates both the Lower Egyptian and Upper Egyptian aspects of the god. The explanation is that this relief affords another example of the artistic convention of combining two independent acts in a single composition see pp. 16, 18 above). On the right, Horus the Behdetite stands on land and mimes the harpooning of the hippopotamus as a summary of what has already happened and as a final demonstration that he is now entitled to be crowned. After the mime he boards his ceremonial bark for the ceremony and finally is acclaimed by the people.

There remains the problem of the two dismemberments of the hippopotamus in Act III. There is nothing here to suggest a double rite, one for Lower Egypt and one for Upper Egypt, and another explanation must be sought. What that explanation may be is never clearly stated. It is perhaps significant that in Act III, Scene i, Horus is depicted but not the king (fig. 14, p. 109) whereas in Scene iii (fig. 16, p. 113) only the Butcher, the Reader, impersonating Imhotep, and the king are shown. This suggests that possibly the first dismemberment was specifically for Horus, and that the second was for the king. Although the triumph of Horus and the gods is proclaimed, it is obvious that it is on the triumph of the king that the emphasis is laid.

It is thus evident that though the wars of Horus and Seth were the framework of the play, the real theme was kingship, in particular the triumph of the king. The play was not merely the mechanical re-enactment of an ancient myth in which Horus defeated his enemy and was crowned as king; the play was the means by which year by year the victory and success of the reigning king, the living Horus on earth, was ensured and through that victory the prosperity and victory of Egypt and her people was also secured. This is why the play begins and ends with the declaration of the triumph of the king and the overthrow of his enemies.

But mythology and kingship are not the only elements in the play. There is another aspect which, though perhaps not immediately obvious, had a profound influence on the form and performance of the play. Seth as the enemy of Horus and murderer of Osiris became a god of evil; he was the god of the deserts and foreign lands and he and his supporters were identified with all the enemies of Egypt, especially with the northerners. The foreign rulers of Egypt realised that one of the cheapest and most effective methods of keeping the people quiet was to support the native cults and priesthoods. This explains the enormous programme of temple building throughout the Ptolemaic Dynasty and the great endowments and privileges accorded the priesthood. The latter naturally appreciated the material advantages that would accrue from at least an outward display of loyalty to the foreign ruler. The special Egyptian conception of kingship and the traditional decoration of the temples made it an easy matter for the priesthood to explain to the king that the elaborate ritual, the great festivals, and especially the majority of the great public festivals, were acts of loyalty to the throne designed to ensure the king's perpetual success and prosperity. The Ptolemies certainly did not understand the underlying symbolism; none of them except for the great Cleopatra,

Cleopatra VI, at the end of the dynasty, even understood the Egyptian language and were content, as long as the country was quiet, to accept things at face value. But the priests were Egyptians, members of a proud race with an age-old tradition of power, influence, civilisation, prosperity and freedom; inwardly very many of them must have resented foreign domination. There is abundant evidence that the native temples were in reality centres of nationalism and that one of the main tasks of the priesthood was to preserve and to fan the spirit of national pride, of nationalism, until the day came when once more the true Horus would sit on the throne.

Mythology and the great annual rituals and festivals of kingship provided the priests with ideal tools in their political, nationalistic propaganda. Outwardly and in theory Ptolemy was represented as the living Horus, the fiction had to be preserved by the ruler and the ruled, but every Egyptian knew that in reality Ptolemy was a foreigner, an enemy. When, therefore, *The Triumph of Horus* was performed each year it was not a mere archaic, religious exercise, it was not solely an occasion for fun and jollity, it was a political act fully understood by the Egyptian audience. All knew that the defeat of Seth by Horus ensured that ultimately not only Egypt's enemies beyond her frontiers but also her foreign rulers should be defeated. Hence the play was designed to be performed in public, before as large an audience as possible. All, actors and audience, were deeply involved; all knew the story and its underlying significance. The audience was not a captive one or a polite, disciplined one, but the deliberately contrived audience participation made the audience as much a part of the play as the actors themselves (see further p. 51 below).

THE AGE OF THE PLAY

Only one copy of the play is known and that, as we have seen, was engraved on the walls of the Temple of Edfu during the first reign of Ptolemy IX, Soter II, approximately in 110 B.C. It is certain that the text was not composed at that time, for scattered quotations from the text are to be found throughout the temple, even in its earliest parts. The complete text of the play must have existed, and the play performed, throughout the entire history of the Ptolemaic temple, whose foundation stone was laid in 237 B.C.

It is impossible to assign precise dates to the earlier history of the play but there is not a shred of evidence to suggest that it was a composition of the Ptolemaic Period; it must have been very much earlier.

This was certainly the claim of the priests of Edfu, for the great horizontal band of inscription over the third register of the west wall of the temple (the wall on which the text of the play is inscribed) states explicitly 'its Wall is inscribed conformably with the Emanations-of-Re' (i.e. the ancient records),[8] and the horizontal band below the first register of the same wall in describing the main features of the decoration of the wall includes both the Legend of the Winged Disk and our play, *The Triumph of Horus*, among them. The Late Egyptian usages that are occasionally to be found in the text of the play suggest that it is a slightly edited and modernised version of a compilation of the later New Kingdom, i.e. some thousand years before the foundation of the Ptolemaic temple. All the available evidence indicates clearly that there was little originality in the inscriptions of the Graeco-Roman temples, except of course the 'historical' texts describing the temple and recording its building history, and religious and ritual texts draw very heavily on older texts, and even on the Pyramid Texts. It is therefore inherently probable that *The Triumph of Horus* was based directly on a much earlier prototype.

The theme of the harpooning of the hippopotamus, which is the foundation of the play, is equally important in any consideration of date. A feast 'Harpooning the Hippopotamus' in the First Dynasty is recorded in the Palermo Stone,[9] though unfortunately nothing is recorded but its name. Thereafter there are frequent references to the ritual harpooning and killing of the hippopotamus[10] from the Pyramid Texts,[11] the Coffin Texts, e.g. after an allusion to the enthronement and coronation of Horus, 'Mayest thou sit in the divine bark when thou harpoonest the hippopotamus in the Winding Lake, every god being thy harpooner',[12] and through the New Kingdom down to the Saite Period. Originally this was a royal ritual, undoubtedly of Lower Egyptian origin; later the theme was adapted and used even in private tombs but it was still perpetuated as a royal ritual. An interesting variant, of which three fragmentary copies have been found in three Theban tombs of the Eighteenth and Nineteenth Dynasties, contains a speech by the goddess Neith to Horus which has obvious parallels with our play: 'Thou hast captured him (the hippopotamus), my son Horus, and art exultant. Thou art triumphant, for thou hast gleamed (after) (*cf.* II.i.88) Nehes (the hippopotamus) in the river. Ho! the harpoon of Horus captures (the hippopotamus)!'[13] The harpooning is also one of the incidents in the New Kingdom story *The Contendings of Horus and Seth*[14] and in the New Kingdom Calendars of Lucky and Unlucky Days.

The literary evidence is also supported by pictorial evidence. The earliest instance known occurs on clay sealings of Udimu, fifth king of the First Dynasty (fig. 2). in which, in the centre, the king in a papyrus

FIGURE 2   King Udimu harpoons a hippopotamus (centre).
Seal impression, Abydos, First Dynasty

canoe and wearing the Red Crown of Lower Egypt harpoons a hippopotamus and on the right wrestles with the monster. The attitudes are so extraordinary, especially the wrestling, that one may be permitted to wonder whether even in the First Dynasty the ritual was so old that it was already mimed. No earlier evidence is known: though predynastic depictions of harpooning a hippopotamus are known, it is not possible to decide whether it is a hunting scene or a religious ritual that is portrayed. Nevertheless, the royal harpooning ritual survived, the most famous example being the superb statuette of Tutankhamun harpooning while in a canoe and wearing the Red Crown.[15]

To sum up the question of date. There is strong evidence to justify the assertion that *The Triumph of Horus* is based directly on a text that, at the latest, was compiled in the late New Kingdom. Whether this text, or a version of it, existed earlier it is impossible to say: in theory it is not impossible but the decisive evidence is lacking. It would seem that a written version or versions of the harpoon ritual was already in existence at least in the early Middle Kingdom. It is certain that a royal harpoon ritual was being celebrated at the dawn of Egyptian history, in the First Dynasty; it was so old or well established that already it was very probably mimed, but we can be certain that at that time there was no written play. *The Triumph of Horus* is therefore based on the central theme of the harpoon ritual, a ritual of kingship and royal victory, that can be traced back unbroken to the First Dynasty, but the written text of the play was compiled at the latest in the period approximately 1300–1200 B.C.

CONSTRUCTION AND RECONSTRUCTION

Although it has been demonstrated that the conflicting theories of Alliot and Drioton concerning the play cannot be accepted, this fact does not automatically imply that the version and interpretation presented in this book are correct. Since there is no single connected copy of the text at Edfu and since it is claimed here that our version is a reconstruction based on a conflation of the evidence of the reliefs and the long inscriptions in vertical columns, it may quite properly be asked what confidence may be rested on such a reconstruction. Is it not another example of modern imagination? Why should it be accepted as an accurate and reasonable version of an actual Egyptian play? We must therefore now attempt to explain how the temple texts and reliefs are to be interpreted, how the present version has been obtained and the guiding rules and principles on which the reconstruction is based.

The foundation of the reconstruction is the fact, which has already been emphasised, that reliefs and inscriptions cannot be divorced from each other but in each scene formed a unit. Every scene in an Egyptian temple was engraved in a precise position, in the only possible place it could occupy in the ritual of which it formed part. Decoration was not foremost in the minds of the priests and sculptors. Often to our modern eyes a relief may appear to be decorative and beautiful but this was not the prime objective of the Egyptians. To the Egyptians the reliefs were engraved for use and for information, the decorative aspect was very far from being dominant. Each relief had the object of giving, subject to availability of space and the conventions of the time, a faithful picture of the appropriate episode or moment in a ritual or a festival. Lack of wall space often necessitated editing and the omission of some episodes but each scene had to be typical, informative, usable and in its exact relative position in the whole ritual. At the dedication of the temple the Ritual of the Opening of the Mouth formed an important part of the ceremonies. It was performed over the temple as a whole, on each statue, on every single relief and inscription in every hall and room. It was repeated annually on New Year's Day at the renewal of the dedication as long as there was a priesthood to perform the ceremonies. The aim was to ensure that the temple, its statues, its reliefs, and the offerings depicted and even the hieroglyphs were imbued with life. It was believed that once the Opening of the Mouth had been performed this latent life was eternal, as long as the building survived, and in theory the rituals and ceremonies could continue even if the temple was abandoned and deserted. This conception of the temple is still very much alive and explains why in tombs and temples one finds that robbers and later occupants have so often attempted to 'kill' the figures by cutting out eyes, ears, nose, mouth, hands and feet.

A second principle underlying our reconstruction is that there must be a consistent and logical rule governing the order in which figures and texts are to be read. One must attempt to discover and respect the Egyptian order. In the inscriptions the order of words and sentences must be preserved, for any attempt to dissect or rearrange texts is inevitably subjective and provides no guarantee that the result of the operation is an accurate reflection of the intentions of the ancient writers.

A few words are also necessary here on hieroglyphic writing. Hieroglyphic texts may be written in horizontal lines or in vertical columns; columns are read from top to bottom, never from bottom to top; and all, whether in horizontal lines or in columns, can be read from right to left (the most usual direction) or from left to right. The direction of reading is determined by the orientation of the hieroglyphs, normally one reads towards the hieroglyphs: if the hieroglyphs face to the right, one reads towards them from right to left. This rule as will be seen, is relevant to the reconstruction of the play. If, for instance, a relief depicts a god who is facing to the left, and if in front of the god there are two columns of text, the first near the god and with hieroglyphs also facing to the left, the second to the left of the first column but with hieroglyphs facing to the right, the first column always records the words of the god and the second contains the words of some other person, usually directly addressed to the god.

At the start of our discussion of the reconstruction of the play it is necessary to point out that the reliefs and main text are not in complete accord. In the reliefs of Act I, as we have already noted (p. 30), two forms of Horus are depicted; in the main text as a whole the text almost always refers simply to Horus, without any further qualification, and the mention of Horus the Behdetite is extremely infrequent except, naturally, in Act III, Scene iii where in the declaration of triumph the full name was essential; in the main text as a whole such emphasis as there is on the person of Horus is on his aspect as a youth, son of Osiris and Isis. The Demons and the Upper and Lower Egyptian Princesses play no part in the main text; the Chorus is never depicted in the reliefs. Except for the boats, there is no indication in the reliefs of the stage or the setting: this, however, is characteristic of Egyptian art at all periods. These differences are very probably not as serious as they might appear. The space available for reliefs and text was extremely

limited and in both there was room only for what was absolutely
essential and in both there must have been a considerable element of
abridgement. Moreover, the reliefs as a whole, but not exclusively,
seem to be particularly concerned with the mimed sections—this is
specially evident in Act I—whereas the main text concentrates on the
spoken words that followed the mime. In general, however, the reliefs
serve the function of a kind of pictorial *dramatis personae* indicating and
identifying some of the principal characters; at the same time they give
some simplified idea of costume and properties. In order to economise
space both reliefs and text complement each other.

The clearest indications of how reliefs and texts are to be read and
combined are afforded by the five scenes of Act I. In figs. 7–11 will be
found detailed drawings of each of these scenes but the omission of the
texts naturally renders the identification of the individual figures and
the disposition of the texts difficult. In fig. 3, therefore, a typical scene
in Act I is represented in simplified, diagrammatic form.

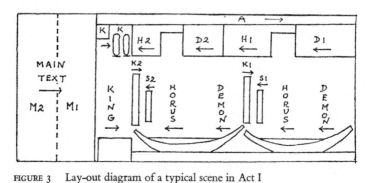

FIGURE 3   Lay-out diagram of a typical scene in Act I
A   Opening Speech of Chorus
DI   Name and Speech of First Demon
D2   Name and Speech of Second Demon
HI   Name and Epithets of Horus Lord of Mesen
H2   Name and Epithets of Horus the Behdetite
K   Cartouches and Epithets of King
KI   King's Address to First Harpoon
K2   King's Address to Second Harpoon
MI, M2   Main Text, First and Second Sections
SI, S2   First and Second Harpoons
Arrows indicate direction in which figures and hieroglyphs face

Each relief clearly consists of two parts. On the left is the main text
in a varying number of vertical columns in which, without exception,
the hieroglyphs face to the right, i.e. the main text must be read from

right to left, the first line of the main text being that immediately behind the figure of the king. On the right is the relief in which are depicted two boats. In the first boat, on the right, stand a Demon and Horus Lord of Mesen, over whom are short columns of text giving (D1) the name of the Demon and a speech uttered by him, and (H1) the name and epithets of Horus Lord of Mesen; in front of Horus a short column (S1) contains words referring to the first harpoon. The second boat, on the left, also has a Demon and over it its name and speech (D2) and Horus the Behdetite, with his name and epithets over him (H2) and a column of text (S2) referring to the second harpoon. Finally, on the extreme left is the figure of the king facing the boats. It will be noticed that whereas in front of the king is a column (K2) containing words of the king referring to the second harpoon, there is no figure of the king accompanying K1 referring to the first harpoon. Obviously the figure of the king has been omitted to save space and we have here yet another example of an apparently single, unitary composition in fact depicting two separate acts. Each relief, therefore, is composed of two parts, the first devoted to the first (or odd-numbered) harpoon and associated with Horus Lord of Mesen, and the second devoted to the second (or even-numbered) harpoon and associated with Horus the Behdetite. It is indisputable that in each scene the action develops from right to left.

One further element in the composition of the relief has yet to be mentioned. Over each relief, but not over the main text, is a single horizontal line of text (A) which has to be read from right to left. There is never any direct indication of the persons to whom the words are to be assigned. The words are usually some form of invocation to Horus but once (I.iii.1–9) the words are clearly direct speech and the pronouns of the speakers are in the first person plural. The same plural pronouns are also employed in II.i.1–11. It is evident therefore that Text A has to be interpreted as the words of a group of people and that these words by their position and orientation are distinct from the rest of the relief. The position of A suggests that it is some kind of introduction or title. We have therefore assumed consistently that it contains the words of the Chorus as the opening of each scene; there is in fact no other position in which these words could logically be placed.

The main text itself needs little comment. The text is continuous, without a break. Usually the speaker is not expressly identified, except by the gender and number of the personal pronouns and by context; there can be little doubt, however, that the identifications in printed translation are correct. Occasionally the next speaker is clearly mentioned and such words have been assigned to the Reader, e.g. 'Isis uttered a cry speaking to the fatherless child battling with Pnehes' (I.iv.22–3). Far more important, however, is the fact that the main text itself falls into two parts divided by the words 'Hold fast, Horus, hold fast' (e.g. I.i.26) assigned to the Chorus and Onlookers. Furthermore, the words preceding this cry (MI) always refer to the first or odd-numbered harpoon and those that follow (M2) always refer to the second or even-numbered harpoon. Each relief and each main text is therefore clearly in parallel; each is divided into two sections, each devoted to a single harpoon. The position of the main text at the extreme left and the direction of the writing strongly suggest that the appropriate sections (MI; M2) have to be read after the parallel sections (A; DI, HI, KI; D2, H2, K2) of the relief.

Such are the facts. In the reconstruction of the play, therefore, each scene begins with A and thereafter proceeds consistently, section by section, from right to left. The printed translation of each scene is thus an almost photographic reproduction of the exact order of each figure and text on the temple relief. Nevertheless, a small element of editorial discretion has had to be used. The texts of the Demons (DI, D2) in the original have the form 'Recitation by' plus Name of Demon plus Speech of Demon. Since some method of identifying each Demon is required by the modern audience or reader, the solution has been adopted of making each Demon introduce himself by substituting the words 'I am' for 'Recitation by'. Alternatively, the name of each Demon might be announced by the Reader, but this does not seem obligatory. Again, the texts HI and H2 consist solely of the names and epithets of Horus Lord of Mesen and Horus the Behdetite; they are certainly not words of Horus and their purpose seems to have been merely a means of identifying and distinguishing the two forms of Horus. Of course, it could be imagined that the words might be uttered by the Reader to announce the speaker, but there is not the slightest hint that the Reader is speaking, each god has already been introduced and identified in the Prologue and we have therefore deliberately omitted HI and H2 from the translation. Finally, the words of SI and S2 are identical with the opening words of MI, M2. Since they are purely repetitive and seem to serve no useful purpose, unless it be as a mark of the transition from the relief to MI or M2 as the case may be, they have been omitted. If it be felt that because these two speeches are given in the relief they should also be repeated in the text of the play, SI should be inserted immediately after the words of the First Demon and S2 immediately after the Second Demon as words of Horus Lord of Mesen and Horus the Behdetite respectively.

The basic principles governing the composition of the scenes of Acts II and III (figs. 12–16) are essentially the same as in Act I, though inevitably there are differences in the characters. All these scenes are therefore to be read from right to left. It will be noted that in Act III, Scene ii (fig. 15) there is no main text to the left of the relief: since this Scene was a mime, the bare minimum of speaking parts was required. In Act III, Scenes i and iii (figs. 14 and 16) Text A, the opening Chorus, is missing. This is less easy to explain. In Act III, Scene iii the available space was extremely limited, a limitation that was only aggravated by the need to find space for extra words and the Epilogue. Thus a possible explanation may be that lack of space dictated the omission of the normal opening words of the Chorus, but this is quite uncertain. In Scene i it might be argued that the two rows of gods left no room for Text A, but on the other hand in Act II, Scene ii (fig. 13) Text A is present in spite of the two rows of women; thus the omission here may well have been deliberate. A definite explanation of these omissions is impossible. Our modern passion for order may lead us to expect that every Scene should have been introduced by the Chorus; the Egyptians may have had other ideas.

It will be readily admitted that, however carefully one may attempt to adhere to the rules that have been established, there must inevitably be points in the reconstruction of an ancient text such as *The Triumph of Horus* where a certain degree of editorial discretion and interpretation has to be exercised. The most important of these points will now be discussed.

The interpretation of the Prologue has presented quite serious problems. At an early stage in preparing the original productions at Padgate it was realised that a modern audience, unfamiliar with the story and the characters, would have difficulty in identifying the actors. It was therefore decided to precede the Prologue by a Parade in which the principal characters were introduced. The Parade was composed by reducing the length of the Prologue and transferring the epithets and words of the characters, with the addition of Horus Lord of Mesen and the Queen who, of course, are not depicted in the relief. It was this version that was used in the production at Padgate and Lancaster.

Such a solution would be inappropriate, even improper, here where we are trying to reproduce the play exactly as it appears at Edfu. Nevertheless, the problem of identification remains. The short vertical columns of text that are over the various persons depicted in the relief (fig. 6) are not speaking parts; they are simply the names and epithets of the persons depicted and their purpose is clearly that of identifying each character. We have thus put each of these texts in the mouth of the Reader: the characters are thus introduced one by one by the Reader and each then recites the brief speech assigned to him or her in the relief. Since, however, the relief does not depict Horus Lord of Mesen or the Queen, though they had important parts to play, we have ventured to insert them in the Prologue. The words of the Reader introducing Horus Lord of Mesen and the words of the god are taken from epithets employed elsewhere in the reliefs, supplemented by a few phrases taken from related texts. The words referring to the Queen are the standard titles of Cleopatra III repeatedly used at Edfu. These inserted passages are printed in italics so that they may be clearly distinguished from the words actually engraved on the wall. Italics are used consistently throughout the translation to indicate words which do not appear in the original. Italics are also used twice, according to normal practice, to mark Egyptian words which cannot be translated and which are given a purely formal transcription, ('*sabet*-snakes' (i.iv.41) and '*deses*-fish' (i.iv.62).

In presenting the characters in the Prologue the principle of working from right to left has been maintained as a general rule but there has been deliberately some deviation in the first part. The relief suggests that the order of the characters would be Isis, Horus, Thoth and the Queen but since we are introducing the characters it has been decided that it would be better to introduce them in relative order of import-ance, Horus the Behdetite, Isis, Horus Lord of Mesen, Thoth, the King and the Queen. From the beginning of the eighth speech of the Reader (Prologue 59) the text translated is that of the vertical columns at the extreme left of the relief and the order of the original is followed with-out deviation. The little hawk-headed figure behind Isis in the boat is that of the god Khentekhtai. Since no words are assigned to him and he plays no part in the drama, he has been omitted. Just why Khente-khtai is depicted here is uncertain but it may be pointed out that he is only mentioned once more in the play (i.v.32) when Isis refers to his having steered a boat; perhaps, therefore, he acted as helmsman.

There are still some other features of the relief of the Prologue that present even more serious problems of interpretation. The most obvious is that Horus is depicted twice, once on land and once in the boat, yet in each instance he is clearly stated to be Horus the Behdetite. Furthermore, the customary horizontal line of text which we suggest (p. 39) is the opening speech of the Chorus does not extend over the whole relief but only over the boat. Finally, behind the figure of Isis at the right of the relief is a single column of text filling the whole height of the relief. This is the only instance of such a line in the 11 reliefs of the play; the text is not assigned to any character and consists solely of epithets and praise of Horus the Behdetite. The explanation of these facts appear to be that yet again this scene is in reality a double one, consisting first of a parade of gods on land and then the embarkation of Horus and Isis on the boat, whereupon Horus, assisted by the King, simulates the harpooning of the hippopotamus which is the theme of Act I. If this be accepted, the vertical column on the right may be interpreted as the words of the Chorus at the beginning of the first section (Prologue 1–7) and the horizontal line, which is to be read from left to right instead of the usual right to left, will be the introduction of the Chorus (Prologue 45–50) to the second part when Horus and Isis board the boat.

Another problem of interpretation arises in Act II, Scene ii (fig. 13). It is a question of how the songs of the two groups of princesses are to be set out. Two groups of women are depicted in two registers, the horizontal line above each group identifying the lower group as the Lower Egyptian Princesses and the upper group as the Upper Egyptian Princesses: these words we have assigned to the Reader. The vertical line in front of each woman gives the words of a couplet, part of a song. How is this situation to be interpreted? In the original English translation in the *Journal of Egyptian Archaeology* each set of words was grouped to form a single song. Another explanation might be that in each group each woman sang a couplet as a solo. Neither of these interpretations is unreasonable but neither seems entirely satisfactory. In Ancient Egypt three is the mark of plurality; the most common method of depicting a crowd is to draw a minimum of three men. Hence, it is extremely improbable that each group of princesses consisted of three women only; it is far more likely that each group was a choir of an unknown number of women. The pronounced parallelism in the couplets (II.ii.38–51) and the Egyptian liking for antiphony suggests that the couplets were sung alternately: this is the solution that has been adopted here.

The last problem occurs in Act III, Scene iii. After the entry of the Butcher a stage direction reads 'Dismembering by the Butcher, Reciting of this book against Seth by the Chief Lector Priest . . . '. 'This book' is not quoted in the text of the play, thus creating an impossible situation for any reader or audience. We have therefore inserted at this point a translation of some extracts from 'The Book of

Overthrowing Apep' which is found in the Papyrus Bremner Rhind in the British Museum. This papyrus was written at the latest in 306 B.C., or perhaps a year or two earlier. The text of the papyrus is lengthy and we have given only an abbreviated selection, but in the same order as in the papyrus (III.iii.16–41). For the benefit of those who may be interested, these extracts have been selected from page 31 of the papyrus. There is, of course, no guarantee that these precise words were used in the Edfu play but we may be quite certain that words very similar were recited.

At various places in the hieroglyphic text there are stage directions. These stage directions are of two kinds. The first kind indicate the name of the speaker. Some are of simple type 'x said': in such instances we have omitted the words; a typical example is Prologue 64 where the original reads 'His Majesty said: "Praise to thee . . . " '. In other examples, however, the name of the next speaker is followed by another phrase: examples are 'Isis, she says to Horus' (I.ii.25); 'Isis uttered a cry, speaking to the fatherless child battling with Pnehes' (I.iv.22–3); 'Isis came, having found the hippopotamus etc.' (I.iv.42–44); 'Isis said to the Young Harpooners when she saw their shapely hands' (II.i.71); 'Isis opened her mouth to speak to her son Horus, saying' (III.i.5): all such passages have been assigned to the Reader.

The second type of stage direction does not indicate the next speaker but states what action is to follow and sometimes indicates the stage properties that are to be used. In all such stage directions the verbal form used is the infinitive, it is quite evident that they were not designed as speaking parts and in a modern play would have simply been printed in italics as a stage direction. If such a procedure were adopted in our play, a modern audience would be completely at a loss to understand what was happening. In the Interlude in Act I, Scene iv, for example, if the action proceeded directly from the last words of the Chorus 'Ye who are in the abyss' (I.iv.40) to the performance of the mimed Interlude, no audience could possibly understand what was happening or realise that it was supposed to mime a mythological happening at Letopolis. All stage directions of this type have therefore been converted into speeches by the Reader, with the minimum of verbal change needed to convert them into direct speech. In addition to the Interlude (I.iv.41) just mentioned, the other examples of stage directions which we have converted into speeches by the Reader are III.iii.9–10. 13–15. 55.

This discussion has been lengthy but necessary. It has demonstrated that the way in which the printed text of the play has been set out owes nothing to the imagination or prejudices of the editor but is the result of a consistent and logical observance of certain definite rules. The reader may be assured that the reconstruction is not a work of fiction or imagination but is an exact transcription of the precise order and words of the ancient document.

STAGE AND ACTORS

The temple of Edfu is on the west bank of the Nile, on the western edge of the modern town and slightly over a mile from the river. All along the west side of the temple are the ruins of the ancient town; to the south are houses of the modern town which tests have shown to be over houses of the Graeco-Roman Period; to the east the modern houses still cover the greater part of the temple enclosure and come to within a few yards of the east wall of the temple (fig. 4). Whether part

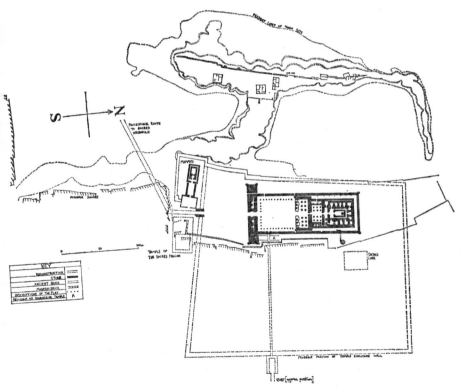

FIGURE 4 Sketch plan of Temple Enclosure and Ancient Town of Edfu

of the ancient town existed to the east of the temple is, of course, unknown. If it did, it would have been to the east of the brick enclosure
wall, and to the east of an ancient canal which must have run roughly
parallel to the wall. The existence of this canal is certain because at the
annual Festival of the Sacred Marriage the bride, Hathor of Denderah,
arrived in her state barge by a canal leading from the river and escorted
by the boats of priests and pilgrims from all over southern Upper
Egypt. It has been suggested that this canal led due west from the Nile
but such difficulties would have been created at low Nile that this is
very unlikely and a canal south to north parallel with the east brick
enclosure wall is more probable. If, therefore, part of the ancient town
existed to the east, the houses must have been at least 150-200 yards
from the temple building. The approximate position of the quay, east
gate and processional route across the sacred enclosure is guaranteed by
the fact that when Hathor arrived from Denderah she entered the
temple by the south-east door of the Forecourt and not by the south
gate of the temenos and the pylons. The French excavations of the
ancient town have shown that in the Ptolemaic Period the street level
to the west of the temple was some 33-35 feet on average above the
floor level of the temple itself.[16] Thus we have to imagine the Temple
of Edfu throughout the Graeco-Roman Period as lying at the bottom
of a huge cup whose rim was formed by the houses of the ancient town.

The exact extent of the sacred enclosure is unknown. Since the
temple itself is very similar to that of Denderah in plan, it has been
assumed that the enclosure at Edfu was probably very similar in area
to that at Denderah, where the brick enclosure wall is preserved.
Similarly the Sacred Lake has been given the same relative position and
dimensions as that at Denderah (Plate 2a). We know from inscriptions
at Edfu, especially the great building texts and descriptions of the
temple, that within the enclosure there were kitchens, abattoirs and a
grove in which the sacred falcons were reared, but there is no hint as to
their position. It may be taken as certain that the enclosure also contained storehouses, administrative offices, houses for the priests on
duty, the House of Life, (a scriptorium) and very probably one or more
small chapels or temples.

How long the ancient town around the temple was in existence is
uncertain. At various points at the foot of the town mound tombs have
been found in the French excavations: most of these date to the Old
Kingdom but some are of the Middle Kingdom. Some of these tombs
have been found approximately 150 yards south-west of the temple,
others about 100 yards due south of the Mammisi or Birth Temple, and

at least two a bare 40 yards due west of the south-west corner of the forecourt of the temple.[17] Clearly in the Old and Middle Kingdoms there was quite an extensive necropolis to the west and south of the area later occupied by the Ptolemaic temple, and in those times no town could have existed there. At an unknown date between the end of the Twelfth or Thirteenth Dynasties and the beginning of the Eighteenth Dynasty this old necropolis was abandoned and a new site brought into use. Only then was it possible for the ancient cemetery gradually to be encroached upon and built upon. This process must have taken some time and one may guess that the development of the town mounds to south and west of the temple is unlikely to have begun much before the beginning of the Eighteenth Dynasty, about 1600 B.C. The excavations in the town mound to the west of the temple have revealed buildings at levels between six and nine feet below the Ptolemaic level: these buildings have not yet been excavated and their date cannot be established. These earlier buildings are evidently some 25 feet above the base line and must indicate a lengthy occupation of the area. This conclusion is reinforced by the fact that to the east of the temple and partly under the east wing of the pylon are the remains of the pylons of a Ramesside temple (fig. 4, A) which can still be seen by any visitor to Edfu: this temple was oriented east to west. The Ptolemaic temple was thus built in part over the ruins of an earlier temple of at least Ramesside times.

This then is the setting and the general history of the site. Where was the play actually performed? The Edfu texts make it clear that in theory the play was supposed to be performed on and around the Sacred Lake, one of whose names was 'Pool of Horus'. It is a reasonable assumption that the lake was more or less identical in position, dimensions and appearance with the Sacred Lake at Denderah (Plate 2a; for approximate position see fig. 4). It was probably about 25 yards by 30 yards, surrounded at ground level by a narrow pavement and low stone balustrade. The sides of the lake were stone-lined, vertical, without sloping mud banks or vegetation. At each corner a flight of stone steps enabled the priests to draw water or cleanse themselves whatever the water level. Texts at Denderah indicate that its Sacred Lake had a small kiosk beside it, though this has now disappeared: very probably there was a similar kiosk at Edfu.

Superficially the Sacred Lake would seem to be the obvious and ideal stage for the play. The east wall of the temple with its registers of brightly painted reliefs would act as a backcloth and sounding board; it is not difficult to imagine the action in boats on the waters of the lake, and the kiosk could well have served as a convenient robing room and waiting room from which the principal characters could make their entrances. Second thoughts, however, raise serious doubts whether, whatever the theory might be, the play could ever have been acted on the waters of the lake and the land surrounding it.

One serious objection is that any performance on the Sacred Lake itself would have reduced drastically the chances of audience participation. Tucked away at the south-east corner of the temple the lake and any performance on or near it would have been completely invisible and inaudible to all people in that part of the town to the west of the temple. The lake would have been visible to only a proportion of the townsfolk to the south of the temple and even only at a distance of between 200 and 300 yards, and the buildings that were in the enclosure must have still further restricted viewers. These are impossible conditions for a great public spectacle. The main purpose of the play would have been largely defeated if the lake had been the stage.

Even more serious objections arise if the practical difficulties and consequences of the use of the Sacred Lake are considered. The lake did not receive direct water supply by pipes or channels from a well, the canal or the river; it was fed exclusively by artesian sources, by seepage. The consequence was that the level of the water in the lake varied enormously throughout the year according to the height of the Nile. During the inundation and for a month or so afterwards the lake would be full but thereafter the level would sink steadily: even in January the level would be several feet below the rim and in the summer months, particularly in May, June and July, the level must have been extremely low, so low that all action on the surface of the water would have been completely out of sight and sound of even actors and spectators within a few feet of the edge of the lake. Doubtless it would not have been beyond the capacity of the Egyptians to have erected scaffolding and thus create an artificial level on which the play could be performed. Such a solution is not impossible but is hardly probable and it at once raises the problem of the hippopotami.

The hippopotami! The imagination boggles at the thought of the unfortunate beasts. It is difficult to understand how live hippopotami could have existed, even for a short time, in such deep water with no foothold anywhere. Who has not heard that hippopotami love 'mud, mud, glorious mud'? One wonders at the problems of supply and producing live animals for each performance. It is even more difficult to imagine how hippopotami could present themselves at the precise moment and the precise position to be stabbed repeatedly by the harpoons of Horus and the King, or how they could be so obliging as to present exactly those parts of their bodies, in due order and sequence, which it was desired to harpoon. We know, of course, that a model hippopotamus in cake was used in the second dismemberment (III.iii.9). It seems certain that a model hippopotamus must have been used not once but throughout the action of the play.

There is slight evidence to suggest that sometimes there were dramatic performances immediately outside the main door in the brick temenos wall of an Egyptian temple. There is, however, no possibility of our play having been staged immediately outside the south gate of the temenos, for there is not the space. A glance at fig. 4 will show that to the west of the gate was the Birth Temple or Mammisi, which still exists; to the east was the Temple of the Sacred Falcon and its enclosure. The latter temple has disappeared completely but five yards south of the east jamb of the south gate of the temenos is a rectangular block of masonry inscribed on all four faces with scenes relative to the cult of the Sacred Falcon; this is probably the lower part of the pedestal of an altar. Further south of this point, at the foot of the town-mound, have been excavated some flooring blocks which apparently mark the south-west corner of a building. The approximate position, therefore, of the enclosure and temple of the Sacred Falcon is reasonably assured.

If neither the Sacred Lake itself nor the area outside the south gate of the temenos could have served as the stage, where are we to look? Admittedly there is no direct evidence, no single trace of a suitable construction to enable us to give an incontrovertible answer to this question. Nevertheless, it seems as though there remains only one place that has the required conditions of space, accessibility and visibility—the court immediately to the south of the pylons. Plate 2b reproduces a recent view of the court and pylons taken from the town mound south of the temple: the camera lens was only a foot or two below the modern street level. If one allows another 20 feet or so to the roof level of the houses, townsfolk and visitors would have had a clear view over the enclosure wall; even at street level it is possible that a view of the play could be obtained, particularly if the performance took place as close to the pylons as possible. In this way a natural amphitheatre was formed, bounded to south and west by the ancient town and the brick enclosure walls and the roof tops afforded excellent vantage points to the townsfolk. The wings of the pylon, which were about 114 feet high, would form an excellent sound-board, and the gigantic figures of the King slaughtering enemies in the presence of Horus the Behdetite

(Plate 2b) would be an appropriate backcloth. We therefore imagine that slightly to the south of the pylons was erected a model of the Sacred Lake, very probably of the same dimensions; model hippopotami and model boats would be used. If it be objected that a model lake could not be the Sacred Lake, it must be pointed out that Egypt was the home of the Creative Word, the word of power (see p. 57); it was sufficient merely to proclaim that the model lake was the Sacred Lake for it to become the real lake; this was normal practice, the Word created. To complete the setting, possibly a temporary kiosk was erected beside the lake, though we have no guarantee that this was so; on either side of the main door in the pylon was a tall obelisk, and in each groove in each wing of the pylon was a lofty mast, wrapped in bands of red, green, blue and white cloth whose loose ends fluttered in the wind. The reliefs, of course, were brightly painted.

The actors and actresses were not professionals and must have been members of the temple priesthood; some of them, for example those taking the parts of Horus, Thoth and the Demons, wore masks. The parts of the King and Queen were certainly played by substitutes, probably senior members of the priesthood. Until Cleopatra VI, none of the Ptolemaic rulers knew the Egyptian language and none appear to have had a direct and personal interest in the native religion. Although the provincial governor often represented the Ptolemaic king at important religious festivals, the language difficulty alone would have prevented him from taking any part in the play. The Chorus would have been composed partly of players present on the stage who filled the role of the supporters and followers of Horus and partly of temple musicians and singers.

Within the temple enclosure and thronging round the lake there was undoubtedly an audience of privileged persons and local notables, who themselves would join in, especially in the cry 'Hold fast, Horus, hold fast!' But the main audience was composed of townsfolk and visitors and pilgrims who crowded every available vantage point, window and roof top. The festivities were not confined to the actual performances of the play. In the town throughout the five days of the festival there would be free food and drink, and endless side-shows, acrobats, dancers, singers and the like day and night. An extract from a text at Edfu describing another popular festival will convey some idea of the atmosphere:

> He (Horus the Behdetite) stands opposite his city, he sees his temple enriched with all its possessions, his city in festivity, its heart rejoicing, all its lanes in gladness. The sound of rejoicing fills its open spaces, all its streets are filled

with exultation, its provisions are more abundant than the sands of the shore. Every kind of bread is in it like sand, long-horned and short-horned oxen are more numerous than grasshoppers. A birdpool for birds is in it. Gazelle, oryx, ibex and their like, the smoke of them, it reaches the sky. The Green Eye of Horus (wine) runs freely in its quarters like the flowing of the inundation from the Two Caverns. Myrrh is on the brazier together with incense, it can be smelled a mile away. It (the city) is bestrewn with faience, gleaming with natron, garlanded with flowers and fresh herbs. The prophets and fathers-of-the-god are clad in fine linen, the king's suite are arrayed in their regalia, its youths are drunk, its citizens are gay, its maidens are beautiful to see. Rejoicing pervades it, festivity is in all its quarters, there is no sleep in it until dawn.[18]

It is in this atmosphere of general gaiety and rejoicing, combined with religious fervour and nationalistic enthusiasm, that the play was performed.

A modern production of the play has inevitably to be staged in a theatre and on a stage of some kind and presented to a passive audience, seated comfortably in rows of seats, polite and well-behaved; an audience that is looking into the stage, detached from the production, unfamiliar with story, setting and characters. At Edfu it was not so. In a sense there was no audience: the onlookers in the town, the privileged audience near the Sacred Lake, the Chorus and the actors were all in, and part of, the play. All knew the story, all understood its significance, all were intensely excited and involved. Hence the greater audience of townsfolk did not simply watch and listen, they did not merely join and supplement the Chorus, they were completely uninhibited and spontaneous. One has to imagine that at almost any moment in the play, but particularly at points of excitement and of tension, there would be completely unrehearsed and spontaneous interventions from the onlookers, excited squeals from children, a man's sudden ejaculation of the name of Horus or of one of the main characters, a curse upon Seth or the hippopotamus, encouragement and incitement of Horus, the ululations of women, even the occasional bray of a donkey and certainly the more frequent barking of dogs.

Such a situation naturally presents any modern producer with extremely difficult problems. In a different age and in a vastly different setting it can hardly be expected that the ideal solution will ever be found, but it must be emphasised that it is essential that some attempt should be made to create the feeling that audience and actors are one, that all are actors and participants, that all are deeply involved, for only in this way can something of the atmosphere of the original play be recaptured.

In such a setting, speeches and acting, to a certain degree, were not the prime essentials. Words, of course, were supremely important: it was the words that brought about the desired effect, the defeat of Seth and the triumph of Horus-King, but as long as the words were recited accurately, it did not matter so much that they were not audible to every onlooker. Obviously the majority of the townsfolk were so far from the lake that they could not have heard many of the speeches. Even if they could hear, it is probable, as we shall see, that to many a large part of the speeches was virtually incomprehensible. It is logical, therefore, to assume that the play must have been designed to have a visual impact.

The general atmosphere and presentation must have been closer to that of a mediaeval Mystery or Morality Play than to any modern drama. There was little action or acting in the modern sense, little attempt to express mood or emotion in expression or gesture. The principal actors probably moved about very little, actions and gestures would be formal, stereotyped and at times exaggerated because of the need for visual appeal. Mime obviously played a large part in the play. Apart from the obvious mimes that formed the Interlude in Act I, Scene iv and the whole of Act III, Scene ii, it is abundantly clear that all the harpooning in the first two acts and the two dismemberments in Act III were mimed. Diction was certainly careful, clear and precise but little expression or emphasis was expressed in speech; the actor would tend to declaim rhythmically, sometimes even to rant.

There is relatively little character drawing but no reader or beholder of the play can fail to be struck by the big part played by Isis. Isis emerges as a very real personality, the dominant character in the play. The text brings out well the two sides of her character: on the one hand the mother acutely anxious about the safety and success of her youthful son; on the other hand, the vengeful, vindictive woman, thirsting for the defeat and death of her husband's murderer.

A few words must be said about music. The only references to music in the play occur in Act II, Scene ii where the Queen says 'I make music for thy pleasure' (II.ii.33) and the Upper Egyptian princesses say 'We beat the tambourine for thee' (II.ii.46). The significance of these words is made perfectly clear by the relief (fig. 13) in which all the princesses are shown beating tambourines and the Queen shakes a pair of sistra. Nevertheless, we may be confident that music did play some part in the ancient production. We can be certain that there was nothing like a modern theatre orchestra, no background or 'mood' music, no overture. We may suspect that music was employed primarily by way of introduction to scenes, to reinforce climaxes, to emphasise and to mark rhythm (see p. 63 below). It is possible also that some at least of the songs may have had a simple musical accompaniment. The final Chorus of Act I, Scene iv (I.iv.70–76), for example, in the Padgate production was taken as a solo, alternate female and male, with an accompaniment on a single flute that was plaintive and haunting, and with at times rhythmical hand-clapping: it was very effective.

The musical instruments used were probably for the most part simple percussion and wind instruments. Among them in all probability were small drums and tambourines; clappers, castanet-like instruments and sistra; flutes and reed pipes. The Egyptians used a number of string instruments, including the harp, but it is doubtful whether they would have been used in the play. Equally uncertain is the trumpet; the Egyptian trumpet apparently had an extremely limited range, the very few notes that could be produced were sharp and harsh; it could not be employed to play a tune and its chief use seems to have been to convey military commands. If the trumpet was used, it must have been confined to a few short and shrill notes at moments of climax.

LANGUAGE AND SPEECH

The translation of the play that is printed below follows very faithfully the original version first published in the *Journal of Egyptian Archaeology:* that version cannot as yet be improved except in relatively minor points of detail. The general style has been 'modernised' very slightly, and with increasing knowledge it has been possible, here and there, to make small improvements to renderings. One or two suggestions made by Drioton have been adopted. A few words which have been destroyed in the original have been restored, but only when good parallels or other good authority exist to justify the restoration. A number of short sentences and clauses are so damaged in the original that no restoration is possible and they have been omitted, on the simple principle that one cannot pronounce a lacuna. By far the greater part of the text is well preserved. It is only in the first speeches of the Chorus (fig. 3, A) that big, and even serious, losses tend to occur; some of these speeches have inevitably been abbreviated. For simplicity's sake restorations and lacunae have not been marked: the reader who wishes to satisfy himself as to the exact state of the text should consult the original English version in which every restoration and lacuna is marked scrupulously.

At only one point is there an addition to previously published translations. In the first entry of the Chorus in Act I, Scene iv there have been added the words:

> . . . whose boundary cannot be overthrown:
> Leader of his company to repel Be;
>
> . . . .
> Ferocious One . . . . (I.iv.6–9)

The extremely fragmentary and damaged state of the text has previously defeated everyone. Renewed and careful study of the surviving traces has made it possible to produce a certain translation in which every word is assured except for the name of Seth 'Be' which is a restoration but not impossible.

In two important respects, however, this version differs from all its predecessors: it differs in combining the reliefs and the main texts, and in setting out the whole play in verse form. The reasons for combining reliefs and main texts have already been explained and discussed but some further comment on the verse form is necessary.

The cardinal difficulties in recovering Egyptian verse are the facts that the vocalisation of the ancient language is lost and that the Egyptians did not normally set out their poems line by line, verse by verse in the manner to which we are accustomed. In many Late Egyptian poems and hymns written in hieratic the ends of the lines of the poem are indicated by red or black verse-points, but in almost all hieroglyphic texts of all periods the individual lines are not marked or separated.

Our present knowledge of Egyptian verse is due almost entirely to the recent researches of Professor Gerhard Fecht. Egyptian never used rhyme, nor a strict metre as we understand it. Metre, if we can call it such, was a matter of stress or beat. The essential element in Egyptian verse was the colon,[19] i.e. a unit composed of one or more words and having a single stressed syllable. The stress for preference fell on the last syllable of the colon, but could sometimes fall on the penultimate syllable. The length of a colon seems to have been determined by grammatical considerations. In pre-Ptolemaic times, at least, the norm seems to have been two or three cola to a line of verse; one colon to a line was rather infrequent; four cola were rare. It is not yet known with any certainty to what extent, if any, the verse scheme of Ptolemaic texts differed from that of the earlier periods.

There are a number of passages in *The Triumph of Horus* that can easily be identified as verse. In our first English translation only two or three of these were printed as verse, the remainder and all the rest of

PLATE I

Act II, scene i

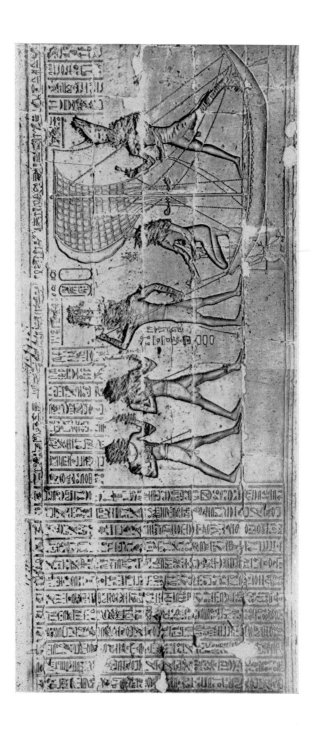

PLATE 2

a Temple of Denderah: The Sacred Lake

b Temple of Edfu: Pylons and Court from the Modern Town

the play were printed as prose. In the intervening years prolonged study of the text and increasing familiarity have bred a growing impression that it is highly probable that the whole play was in verse. This is an impression only, which is as difficult to prove as to disprove: some there will be who will disagree with this interpretation. Nevertheless, it has been decided that the attempt ought to be made to present the whole play in verse form. It must be stressed, however, very strongly that though the translation is accurate, the attempt to present it in verse is frankly experimental. It would take many months, perhaps years, of concentrated effort to produce a verse version that could be claimed to be final and definitive and time for this is, alas, at present not available. The present verse form, therefore, lays no claim to be more than an honest but experimental approximation: in due course it may very well and legitimately be profoundly modified.

Two further points ought to be made. First, in attempting to turn the translation into verse a very strong attempt has been made to be impartial and not to be influenced by any preconceived prejudices, apart from adherence to rules and a personal feeling of the demands of construction and context. When the final draft was completed, and only then, it was surprising to note the unusually high proportion of lines with four cola. This may simply mean that, at times at least, the pattern of the verse is wrong; it may, however, mean that verse of the Graeco-Roman temples contained a higher proportion of lines of four cola than the poems and hymns of the Middle and New Kingdoms. Only a study in depth of the numerous hymns that are to be found in the inscriptions of the Graeco-Roman temples will decide this point.

Secondly, the nature of the long declarations of the triumph of Horus, the gods and the King and the overthrow of their enemies is uncertain, particularly in Act III, Scene iii and in the Epilogue; so also the names and titles of the King that occur from time to time throughout the play. Some there may be who will feel that all these also ought to be in verse; this is not impossible. Rightly or wrongly, however, it has been decided that all such passages ought to be presented as prose. It is imagined that they were spoken or intoned as a form of rhythmical recitative.

The hieroglyphic text presents many of the literary and stylistic forms so characteristic of Egyptian literature. Alliteration and verbal puns are frequent; parallelism of members and antiphony is employed occasionally: similes and metaphors are common. Alliteration is extremely common in Ptolemaic texts; in the play it is not as frequent as in developed ritual texts of the time but it is a prominent feature of the play: it is unfortunate that no English translation can possibly convey this alliteration. On the other hand, every effort has been made to render the puns, as far as is possible.

The language of the play is essentially classic Middle Egyptian, but it is not pure Middle Egyptian. The language is really a debased form of Middle Egyptian that is so characteristic of the temples of the Graeco-Roman Period that it might be termed, to coin a new phrase, 'Temple Egyptian'. It is bastard Middle Egyptian with some contamination by Late Egyptian and even, occasionally, by Demotic. In the text of the play there are a few Late Egyptianisms, but it is characteristic of Edfu that they are not as frequent as in the inscriptions of the temple of Denderah, for example. The vocabulary also contains a proportion of new words or, at least, new nuances of words that are unknown in Middle Egyptian or Late Egyptian, in Demotic or even Coptic. They might be new inventions, but this is somewhat unlikely because they apparently have no future. Possibly the temple scribes were deliberately exploiting and reaching back to very ancient and early sources of vocabulary and material that are now completely lost to us.

The point is an important one. From the point of view of the average Egyptian of the Ptolemaic Period the language of the play was archaic. The hieroglyphic writings and spellings of words reflect a conscious effort to render the contemporary pronunciation but a proportion of the vocabulary and all of the grammar were not that of contemporary, Ptolemaic Egypt. It is probable that to all but an elite of senior priests and scribes the play was to a very large extent incomprehensible, more even than Chaucer is to many people today. To us this may seem an extraordinary situation. The explanation lies partly in the fact that the play was an ancient, sacred drama, but even more in the Egyptian conception of the Word. It did not matter if the words of the play were incompletely understood by the audience provided that the ancient, traditional words were uttered correctly and without omission, for the Word was all powerful, the mere utterance of the ancient words was sufficient to create the desired end, the triumph of Pharaoh and of Egypt.

Such a situation presents obvious difficulties to the translator. There is no justification for translating Egyptian texts of any period into the English of the Authorised Version of the Bible; but it would be equally and completely wrong to render the play in a completely modern idiom. The position is further complicated, as we have just seen, by the fact that the whole play was deliberately written in an archaic idiom. In our translation, therefore, a deliberate attempt has been made to convey the archaic nature of the hieroglyphic text: the vocabulary used has been chosen with care to give some indication of the flavour and weight of the original words. We have also used deliberately 'thee' and 'thou', as a mark of respect when a god or a superior character is addressed, and 'ye' is usually employed for the plural 'you' in order to avoid ambiguity.

It is inevitable that the vocabulary and names in the play should offer real difficulties to the modern reader and speaker. It cannot be emphasised too strongly, however, that to an Egyptian the word, especially in religious ceremonies, was of supreme importance. The word indeed was the Creative Word: to name a thing was to create it, to give it substance and reality; to deny a thing or a crime was sufficient to make it non-existent. This is why an Egyptian never confessed to having sinned. This explains why in the famous Denial of Sins in Chapter 125 of the Book of the Dead a man, though he might have committed a dozen major crimes, had only to deny having committed them to be declared innocent. The efficacy of religious ceremonies depended less on belief and understanding than on the ritual purity of the officiant, the correct performance of the manual rite and the complete and unswerving accuracy of the spoken words. In the Edfu play words and diction, not 'acting', were paramount.

In a modern performance, therefore, the words, however difficult, are important. As we have already said, they were declaimed, without overmuch emphasis or stress, at a fairly constant speed; speed could lead to slurring of words and hence to loss in their efficacy.

Throughout the translation the Greek forms, where they exist, of proper names have been used, since they represent pronunciations that at one time were actually used, though admittedly they were late forms. For personal and place names that have no Greek equivalents formal, conventional vocalisations have been employed. In all such Egyptian words the stress is always on the last or on the penultimate syllable. Thus 'Amun' is correct and not 'Amen' wherever the name of the god stands alone or is the last element in a name, as in 'Tut-ankh-Amun'; when Amun is at the beginning of a word, it is short, as in 'Amen-re'. Similarly, Mesen, not *Meesen, should be used. *Kh, tj, dj* are single sounds; *kh* is pronounced like *ch* in Scottish 'loch' and not as *k* as is so often done in English. *Th* as in 'thing' does not exist in Egyptian and must be pronounced as two separate letters, hence 'Hat-hor' not 'Hathor'. Lastly, *h* almost always is a hard breathed sound: in 'Behdet', for instance, the English tendency is to pronounce it as *Bedet, often with a slight hiatus before *d*; the correct pronunciation is Behdet, with *h* strongly breathed. 'Behdetite' will probably need considerable rehearsal!

3 The Production of 'The Triumph of Horus'

Derek Newton & Derek Poole

If 8 May 1956 with the first production of John Osborne's *Look Back in Anger* can be generally acclaimed to be a significant date in the consideration of contemporary British Theatre, it could be said that 23 June 1971, with the presentation by Padgate College Department of Drama in Education and Theatre Crafts of Professor Fairman's *The Triumph of Horus*, was of even greater importance in an assessment of the development of World Drama. Professor Allardyce Nicoll (who should know) said in a letter to Padgate that 'this was an important occasion as, so far as I am aware, it is the first attempt to "revive" any ancient Egyptian ritual play'. It is interesting to note that Professor Nicoll used the word 'ritual'—the very word that in the beginning inhibited our thinking of anything in the way of a theatrical performance.

Now in 1973 our initial fears seem groundless. But how, the reader may rightly demand, did Padgate College of Education, a college of some 1,000 potential teachers, become involved in a theatrical and dramatic event of this nature? The answer—By chance.

In 1968 Professor Fairman's daughter Jennifer joined the College as a student of Drama, Physical Education and Education to read for the B.Ed. degree. A chance remark from the Head of the Department of Drama in her second term that 'I don't suppose your father has got any Ancient Egyptian plays tucked away in a drawer at home?' produced the surprising, and now historic, answer of 'Yes'.

The first script of *The Triumph of Horus* was brought to the College as part of a collection of transcripts of other reliefs. The script of the play with language and terms and proper names of strange delight produced but thoughtful alarm as a potential stage presentation involving several years of enthusiastic students of Drama and Theatre in Education.

How did we proceed? After a period of unproductive thought Mr Geoffrey Raymond, a member of the Departmental staff, was asked to produce the piece with a group of second-year students as a play for radio. To Professor Fairman's script was added an additional narrator and the programme was completed by using our studio radio equipment. The result was not disappointing. It sounded, with well-mixed background sound effects, as a good pre-war schools broadcast might have done. 'Echoes from the Past', 'The Sounds of History' might well have been titles of the series in which it was put out.

If the radio play highlighted some of the problems, it did not solve them. At this time (1970) we did not see the initial theatrical simplicity of the play. It was from this point on that the text, coupled with our ignorance of the Egypt of the period, caused us to contemplate a production on closed circuit television only, using filmed extracts of actions with the protagonists at times appearing in shot and otherwise being used as 'voice-over' action, that would have included shots of the Edfu reliefs and other stills of Ancient Egypt. (Readers may be aware of some of the filming that has been done in this manner, e.g. Dante's Inferno, Hieronymus Bosch.) Later, having felt this to be an unsatisfactory method of launching Professor Fairman's text on the world, we considered the possibility of an outdoor arena production—but still with an element of back projected scenes—done at dusk and using some of the flat roofs of the Padgate Campus for Hollywood-epic processions and descent over the heads of an unsuspecting and possibly chilled audience.

An assessment of noise from the campus and the Motorway caused us not to proceed.

We returned to a contemplation of photographs of the Edfu reliefs, the simplified line drawings and the text. These, together with photographs of temples similar to that at Edfu, provided an answer to methods of production. This study, together with a remark from Professor Fairman that 'this play should have no bogus air of solemnity', reassured us all and enabled us to commit to production.

Small groups of students worked together with tutors on all aspects of the presentation.

CREATING THE FIRST PERFORMANCE

Rehearsals started a fortnight before the June 1971 production opened. This was the period after final examinations had been completed for many of the students involved. A group of fourth-year students who had finished their course were to play the most demanding roles and were available for full-time rehearsals as necessary. Second-year and first-year students, who were to make up the Chorus, Crowd, Young Harpooners, Demons, Princesses and Gods, were only available some of the time during the day. The greater part of their work was carried out in evening sessions.

As part of our policy it has been usual to carry out short and demanding periods of rehearsal before a presentation. A major educational project can be carried out with various teams concerned with, for example, costume, properties, scenic design, carrying out their work under the control of student coordinators who in their turn are responsible to staff direction. With a few exceptions all students had an area of Theatre Crafts in which to work apart from their performance commitment.

Small groups under student Directors created the sequences such as the Interlude of the *Sabet*-snakes and the movement and action, like the Young Harpooners, around sections of the play that could be removed from main rehearsals. June Fortune looked after rehearsals concerning the main characters. Positions were largely to be static, so maximum time was devoted in the first week to running and learning lines. There had to be accuracy in each line to an exact degree. Rehearsal could not progress until all matters dealing with pronunciation had been satisfactorily resolved. It was then a question of mechanical learning for each individual.

Perhaps the biggest problem of rehearsing the main roles arose from the fact that the characters in the play are not characters in the traditional sense, so that the student actors were in the strange position of attempting to be unsophisticated actors playing priests and priestesses who were playing Kings and Queens. A strong declamatory style was needed that also had to convey a feeling of joyful commitment. There had to be urgency and pace that still maintained careful articulation. The level of projection had to be strong. This main group had a lonely and unrewarding task until all the elements of the play came together on the Sunday afternoon of the weekend before production. At that session, for the first time, there was a feeling of satisfaction and of being concerned in a major piece of educative theatre. The leading players found their rehearsal sessions physically tiring to a greater extent than usual. For most of the time they remained in a static posture changing only the position of their arms and head. Their only physical relief was in some of the major changes of place and attitude that took place between the scenes. Even here the tension that their words and performances had created could not be broken. The play was felt to be a reversal of all their drama in education training. There was no question of being able to use modern methods of actor involvement.

Intense personal discipline was required. This discipline appeared to hold their audience both in and outside the play. It was obvious that the Chorus, if only by the number of lines given to it, fulfilled a vital role in the play. It was equally obvious that the chorus members could not have been an *ad hoc* collection of individuals but were most likely associated with the temple and possessed of certain dramatic skills—perhaps mime, dance, and music; but exactly what their corporate role was it was not at first easy to understand from the printed page, for the play dealt with a mythology and culture imperfectly understood by us. But whatever the role, and at first it seemed to be one centred largely around praising Horus, it was clear that there were moments of violent physical action and moments of pure lyricism, which must have been achieved by dance, music, song, and speech. But what dance? What music? What song?

Many of the students had earlier worked in a production of Euripides' *The Bacchae* which had been placed in a modern idiom, and the music and dance which we had then evolved had been successful and had in no way violated the principles of Classical drama whilst being obviously different from the originals—and who really knows exactly how a Greek Chorus sang and danced and used choral verse? If this presentation had been aesthetically valid, why not apply the same principles to *Horus*? Accordingly we listened to records of Middle Eastern music, we looked at illustrations of flute players and dancers, we talked of movements we had used in *The Bacchae*, of religious ritual that we knew of or were familiar with, of processions, pageants and song, and realised that we had to catch a flavour of the Egypt of the period, and not try to achieve an exact similitude. Because we had worked together before, it was possible to look at every instance of Chorus involvement and, having decided on its purpose, to allow all to be free to suggest how it might be done. Thus, a liturgical type chant by the director having been vociferously rejected as 'doleful' and too 'Churchy' was altered by a student with marked musical ability and became an impressive entrance chorale for the Chorus's first entrance suggesting the type of movement to be used. This entrance was from the upper stage, the opening line 'The King of Upper and Lower Egypt' being sung off stage, and solo voices singing part lines as the Chorus processed down stage and descended the steps to the main Chorus area ending—when all were in position as part of a semi-circle facing the stage—with a slow kneeling obeisance. This created an appropriate atmosphere for the opening speech of the Reader.

Similarly a beautiful lyrical melody composed by the same student led to accompanying movements being evolved by a student with a deep knowledge of Dance, and to the introduction of a flute accompaniment.

We had researched into the types of musical instruments used in Ancient Egypt and had decided that apart from a single flute we would use percussion instruments. These could be employed in many ways— to accentuate rhythm, to assist sound climaxes, to underscore certain lines and passages, to punctuate—and they were simple to make as they have been all through history. Bottles, jars, tins, all suitably disguised, were filled with a variety of materials; sistra were made by using forked twigs similar to catapults and threading bone and metal discs on wire which joined the extremities of the forks. They made very interesting sounds. We also used a single drum of the 'tom-tom' type. Instruments that were unacceptable, usually because of the type of sound they created, were quickly discarded until we were left with the flute, the drum, several sistra, one or two 'shakers', and a finger-operated device that was in effect a small bell. It was not the making of instruments we found valuable, but their uses, which stimulated a flow of ideas leading to the creation of more movement, different sound and speech patterns, and as people began to be more proficient in using instruments so they began to find more uses for them.

In this way of working, a corporate rather than a directed method, a profound involvement was achieved, and the functions of the Chorus began to be more numerous and more significant as they created, through their discipline and integrity, the blood and muscle to activate the bare skeleton, the script. Physically the Chorus was separated both from the stage level used by 'characters' and from the Crowd, as was the Chorus in post-Classical Greek tragedy. This, it was thought, would probably have been so in early productions, and it enabled the Chorus at times to distance themselves from action and by so doing develop and strengthen atmosphere. An example can be found in Act I, Scene i. The Chorus speech (i.i.16–25) following the line of Horus Lord of Mesen—'The blade takes hold in the head of the Hippopotamus in the Place of Confidence'—comes after a powerful Demon entrance and before a second Demon speech, which is also powerful and very bloodthirsty; the Chorus section between the speeches was played in a restrained manner with girls' solo voices, each taking a natural section and ending fairly quietly with a restrained chant of 'Hold fast, Horus, hold fast', the intention being to counter the First Demon's speech by restraint, to pave the way by contrast for the second more violent outburst, and to enable the Chorus to reserve their power for their second contribution to the scene on the line 'Grasp firmly the harpoon (1.i.36). This section was largely carried by the four male members of the chorus who combined solo voices and vigorous mimetic movement, the girls contributing to the final crescendo and to 'Hold fast, Horus, hold fast'.

A word should perhaps be said about the recurring line 'Hold fast, Horus, hold fast'. Its purpose does not always seem to be the same. It acts sometimes, we felt, as a seal to a section of the action; it appears sometimes to be a cry of encouragement, sometimes of exhortation; occasionally it merely closes or rounds off a chorale, and sometimes it might be a shout of exultation. It became for us a chant, soft and gentle at times, often urgent and backed by percussion; or a unison shout; or sometimes a solo voice, almost a reflective chant, as at the conclusion of the Isis speech at the end of Act I, Scene iii, which we conceived as a piece of lyrical poetry. But from Act II onwards we brought in the voices of the crowd, at first quietly, hesitantly joining in as though feeling their way, until they participated fully, and the familiar line was given a volume and significance so that it linked characters, Chorus and Crowd in one complete whole. But the Chorus was not solely a 'choir' of singers or speakers, nor were its movements all stylised, and when the line appeared to demand it the Chorus 'individualised' and both vocally and physically worked to and with the Crowd.

It had seemed to us that the Chorus did not play merely a static role in the ritual. Certainly they were there to praise, to fill in the picture as in Act I, Scene i, in the speech beginning 'Grasp firmly the harpoon' (1.i.36) in which also they appear to explain and even teach; but at times they appear to share some of the prophetic vision of a Greek Chorus. It is interesting to note how often a scene is opened by the Chorus, with the exception of Act III, Scenes i and iii (see further, p. 41 above), as though they formalised or led the act of worship. Equally they bring each scene to a conclusion. This 'framing' of scenes by the Chorus enabled us to transfer attention to the harpoon ritual naturally and effectively, but in Act III, with the exception of Act III, Scene ii, the Chorus does not open, its role appears to change. Even in Act II, Scene i, although it opens, the Chorus does not merely lead the praise, but apparently leads to a different locale, in our presentation to the upper stage, and from this point onwards it might appear that the Chorus becomes less and less formal, more actively engaged in violent emotion. This is not, of course, a sudden change. The final lines of the preceding Act (1.v.42–46) are not exactly tranquil:

Seize ye and lay hold, ye lords of strength;
Plunder, ye masters of savage beasts!
Drink ye the blood of your foes and of their females;
Sharpen your knives, whet your blades,
Steep your weapons in the blood!

but it seemed to us that the Chorus now begins to work directly on the crowd.

In some ways the role of the Chorus is analogous to that of the Lector-Priest; he appears to have been not only a Priest, but a Priest charged with the task of production, responsible not only for ensuring that the Triumph of Horus is performed, but that the performers carry out their functions properly, and he appears on stage with them, as a Priest and also as a director, controlling them and the action; 'Seth has been judged in the Tribunal of Re and Thoth says:', or, 'Isis said to Horus:', or simply a statement, 'Adoration of the Sacred Harpoon'. In practice our Lector Priest gave every cue—like the original Priest he had to know everything that was to happen.

It seemed that the Chorus, too, must know more than its own part. It had had to lead the audience, sometimes perhaps physically as when in Act II, Scene i the opening line is 'Come, let us hasten to the Pool of Horus . . . ', sometimes by indicating the nature of the response the crowd could make. For example, in Act II, Scene ii, in which the people acclaim Horus crowned and invested with the emblems of Kingship, the Chorus, already on the upper stage and in close proximity to the crowd, turned to the onlookers and led them in the cry 'King of Upper and Lower Egypt for ever!' (II.ii.30)—an action which seemed to us natural since the preceding action of Horus in assuming the Double Diadem and overthrowing the foe marked a climax in the play and ceremonial. Similarly at the beginning of the same scene the joining together of the crowd and Chorus in an outburst of joy on the line 'Horus has taken possession of the throne of his father' (II.ii.12) again marked a climax, though a rather different one, for the Chorus here does not rejoice after the accomplishment of an act but is employed as a characteristic device, found in the literature of many countries, to declare the result of an act that has yet to be performed.

The Chorus, then, as Mr Poole saw it, acquired a dual role; it took a direct part in the play, itself creating and developing atmosphere, sometimes lyrically and gently, sometimes processing to the upper stage with dignity, sometimes surging into position, but it also turned figuratively and literally away from the play; by leading and exhorting the crowd it brought them in to the action and by stimulating the emotions added to the intensity of that action. If it were assumed that the onlookers would be familiar with some of the text, as today we are familiar with parts of Hamlet, or as a Mediaeval crowd in Chester might be familiar with some of the lines in the Crucifixion, then their participation would be both possible and natural, perhaps inevitable. This assumption was made, and the effect of the Crowd's involvement was very powerful, as, for example, in the Interlude which forms Act III, Scene ii:

> *Chorus:* The noise of rejoicing resounds in Mesen,
> Gladness issues from Behdet,
> For Horus has come that he may slay the Nubian,
> And his confederates in the place of slaughter.
> He has cut off his head,
> He has cut out his heart,
> He has drenched him in his own blood.
> Wetjeset-Hor and Denderah are in jubilation,
> Alack, alack in Kenset! (III.ii.1-9)

The Crowd began to join in on line 5 building to a vocal climax on the last line, and also to a climax of urgent movement, whilst the Chorus, standing below the Crowd, whipped them into a near frenzy. The last line, although apparently stating a measure of regret, we treated as a shout of triumph. Similarly, in the following scene, The Second Dismemberment of Seth, the Crowd added its power to the Chorus lines in the section following the cutting up by the butcher of the hippopotamus-shaped cake.

Professor Fairman has said that the Crowd was important; it would see the play not only as a religious occasion but as an affirmation of national pride, and it would participate spontaneously; the text and the action confirm this, and as the Chorus worked first with the characters and then with the Crowd, the three elements coalesced and through interaction began to create an atmosphere that removed the play from a typical twentieth-century concept of Theatre and revealed elements of exaltation and violence of almost Bacchic nature. Isis, at once caring-Mother and seeker of vengeance, had her violence fed back to her by Chorus and Crowd, finding it difficult to stay within her range of patterned movement, and the director began consciously to stylise the violence of both Chorus and Crowd lest it destroy the form of production that had been evolved. At the end of the play the Crowd, purged of violence, slowly dispersed and the Chorus made a slow processional exit from ground level up to upper stage and thence off, chanting as they processed, and leaving behind them, gradually fading on the air, the sound of a single female voice singing a soft incantatory pattern. There was some kind of Catharsis.

STAGING

We decided to convert our proscenium into a 'temple' area and to use the stage area behind the proscenium as the 'lake'. As most of the action on the 'lake' was to be visual, the main acting areas for the Reader and the other leading characters were down-stage of the proscenium arch on the apron stage.

In front of the apron stage, tiered rostra and steps brought us down to the floor of the auditorium itself. Further rostra and treads were used to project thrust stages left and right of the proscenium arch.

On the Padgate Drama Studio stage there is an 18-foot-diameter revolve. We moved the side sections and used the circle as the lake surface itself. For the second production at Lancaster we constructed a rectangular lake of low block rostra.

Above the projecting stages left and right, platforms eight feet above stage height were constructed for the crowd of Egyptian people who were to be so important to the development of the action. Secure above the main acting areas they were able to be part of the ritual on stage as well as to be involved in the work and movement of the chorus.

The acting areas in front of the proscenium, under the high levels and the semi-circular floor area, were covered with foam-backed carpet underlay used upside down. This covering was painted in the same manner as the general setting. This soft surface was splendid for movement with bare-footed actors and had a physical warmth that affected the whole body.

Access to the upper levels was by ladders. The auditorium area had a solid altar-piece in the centre.

Figure 5a shows a sketch view of the method of presentation, while fig. 5b shows it in ground-plan form.

The proscenium arch and side walls were covered over with a base material stuck directly to the brick work. These surfaces were then decorated with a design created by the partial use of detail from the Edfu reliefs and free interpretation of some of the symbols used in them. Instead of using conventional methods of 'squaring-up' from small designs we photographed some of Professor Fairman's photographs and drawings on to 35mm transparencies. These slides were then

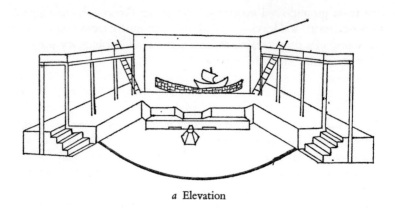

a Elevation

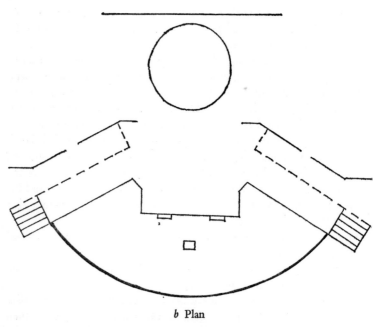

b Plan

FIGURE 5   The Stage for the Padgate production

projected on to the walls and the required detail drawn round. Next the drawn lines were gouged out to a half-inch depth. Thus we gained 'relief' in what was our basic scenery, that was very responsive to changes in lighting. In Plate 3a and the right side of Plate 4b the effect can be seen. The 'lake' edge in Plate 3a is deserving of comment. This is made of large garden 'walling' blocks. After painting we not only had an interesting texture but a firm foot-wide surface to stand and move on. This circular pathway was used in Act III, Scene i for the appearance of the Gods, as it was used also for the Young Harpooners and for the Demons. It was of great advantage in the change-over from scene to scene.

We played *The Triumph of Horus* without interval. The action was continuous, but each change of scene in the text was marked by a fade to silhouette as near as possible to the scene shown on the original reliefs.

The white plastered cyclorama upstage of the revolve was used with strong saturated colour effects. Batten lighting circuits in blue, red and green were mixed in with contrasting colours projected by lanterns focused directly on the centre. By taking out all front lighting we saw black silhouette outlines against colours that matched the developing violence and the later triumphant mood of the play.

In silhouette the boats moved, the sail was brought on, the hippopotami were held up, the stabbings took place, the characters adjusted. In Plate 3a the scene is just about to move in as the lighting has come up after silhouette sequences have ended.

The walls, the floor, the edge of the lake were coloured in a very rich yellow amber with the plain colour broken by grey, light brown and light red areas 'splattered' from wide brushes to produce a 'mincemeat' effect.

A vivid outdoor look was necessary, while at the same time, it was proper to avoid extravagances of scenic detail. Both at the Padgate and Lancaster Theatre Studios the audience walked into what appeared to be, within the limits of their knowledge, Ancient Egypt. As the auditorium lighting faded and the live musical sounds swelled out the 'Crowd' who started the play walked into a total environment. Without this form of setting the task for young and inexperienced students would have been too great to sustain.

Likewise the audience might not have been conditioned to accept the action and the hypnotic strangeness of the event. In an inexplicable manner the physical setting only came really alive after the first music had been heard. Apart from the instruments used by the Chorus mentioned earlier there were live 'musicians' to introduce the action and in particular to cover the silhouette changes. At Padgate they were high up in the fly tower above the stage, while at Lancaster an original stereophonic effect was created by placing the musicians on catwalks of the lighting grid above the heads of the audience. The instruments, oil drums, steel baths, hosepipes trumpeted into plastic drain pipes of various diameters, were obviously not authentic. Their resonant and insistent notes and rhythms were, as one newspaper put it in a complimentary manner, 'out of this world!'. It was this necessary removal from our world that affected all our decisions concerning the staging of the play.

A great deal of equipment was employed to produce the broad lighting that we used to achieve the effects at Padgate. At Lancaster, where the lanterns were much stronger in output, we found that we needed less equipment than used there normally in order to isolate our temple walls and lake so that they appeared to float in a warm tone isolating the rest of the large studio in total darkness.

The lighting plot was simple. At times adjustment was made to focus on action and at other moments, with for example the demons and the dancer, the main lighting was brought down in strength and a strong contrasting colour was inserted into the general warm sunlit effect. It was perhaps more a technique of British traditional pantomime than of Ancient Egypt but it appeared to succeed in adding to visual excitement and concentrating the attention and response of the Chorus and Crowd.

Up to a very late stage in the June 1971 production we contemplated using special effects lanterns to simulate moving waters on the lake and to give an effect of turbulence in lighting to match certain sections of the text. We also had slides to project on the cyclorama. These were to be used as 'cut-ins' are in film. While the Chorus were approaching a verbal climax we had envisaged flashing shots of Egyptian faces in matching attitudes, shots of the hippopotamus, shots of the temple.

This was a vestige of the approach we contemplated in 1970. It took only the first run-through of the play to realise finally that Professor Fairman's text coupled with the attack of our cast made the superfluities of much of the theatre of our own decade far from necessary.

It was a similar lack of confidence in what we can now see as the basic simplicity of the play that had misled us into complicated thoughts concerning the properties. From the reading of the text it will be seen that certain properties are central to the concept of the staging of the play. For a long time we had deluded ourselves by thinking in terms of naturalism and simulated reality.

The boats in the relief seemed to be small vessels floating—the hippopotami to be animals . . .

PLATE 3

a Padgate: General view
of the set, showing the
'Lake' and positions for
main characters and
crowd

b Padgate: Act III,
scene iii: The Butcher
cuts up the hippopotamus
cake

PLATE 4

a Padgate: Chorus comes from the stage area to lower acting area

b Padgate: The Chorus rejoice: Isis centre, King left centre, Queen right

Just before the rehearsal period of the original production was to start a group of student workers came to a realisation. Discarded now were ideas of articulated figures, hoisted sails and blocks. They saw that if we thought in terms of two dimensional cutouts, the play would work. It was then that we thought of a hobby horse and other token methods of acceptable presentation in English folk drama. More than being acceptable it seemed historically possible. Here was a staging method of basic ritual drama. With a verve that could possibly parallel the enthusiasm of Archimedes the boats, the hippopotami, the bound captive, the goose were designed. When these cutouts, all two inches in thickness, were brought into the action it seemed that we were right. Finally the only properties that had any resemblance to realism were the chalice for feeding the goose in Act III, Scene iii, the scroll held by the Reader and the cake shaped like a hippopotamus. Here we decided that a new hippopotamus cake for each performance was not appropriate, so a hollowed part of the back was used as the container for the morsels of cake that were thrown to the waiting crowd.

Costume and wigs evolved in a similar way to the properties. Working with a group of six students we created costumes on draped lay figures and then transferred them to people to allow movement 'trials' to be undertaken. This stage was both photographed and filmed. For costume design we used all sources that we could find but, finally, it was a book for children in the 'Ladybird' series that helped us most both with choice of colour and with practicality. The Crowd basic costumes were of rough off-white material, the Chorus silver-grey, semi-transparent light textures worn over body stockings while the protagonists were in thin materials of primary colours of reds and blues. The Reader was in silver and gold and his servants in rich purple. Here we chose to discard authenticity and concentrate on what we knew would create imposing pictures against the tonality of the setting and the richness of the lighting. Head-dresses were authentic in shape and were fitted individually to each character.

One chance of fortune probably secured the visual success of the production. Some months earlier the Department had purchased the complete contents of a Manchester dress-trimming shop that provided us at a low cost with hundredweights of metal buckles, buttons, belts and trimmings that gave us exciting raw materials that were receptive to light. These materials were of particular use in creating head gear, arm bands and pectorals. The weight problems when the prototypes were transferred from lay figures to people were considerable, but were resolved.

On inspection, Plates 3 and 4 will give some impression of the ways in which the various costume accessories were used.

The plates also show the wigs. By the end of the two productions we had nearly 100 wigs, made of dyed mop material, that had been individually built on head shapes. Special characters, for example Isis, had a wig and head-dress built as one, then painted and decorated.

The wigs, accessories and indeed the stylised make-up treatments did not bear the close-up inspection of the film camera, but at the 'viewing' distance we had chosen the illusion was complete.

What of the first production? One local theatre critic said 'it was an experience to watch, for the play systematically and ritualistically sketched the intensity and cumulative atmosphere of an ancient ceremony . . . the play was structurally beautiful—the clockwork timing of painted puppets mouthing the words of their historical counterparts; the soft lyrical quality of the choruses, the vitally simple lines on which play was even made possible, for in using toys as symbolic beasts a major problem of production was overcome.' Another, writing in the *Manchester Evening News*, said, 'as a piece of theatre it was an experience not to be missed by anyone interested in the foundations of drama—an hour and ten minutes of allegory enacted with exemplary discipline and dedication by a cast of 70.'

THE SECOND PRODUCTION

During the first production we had recorded the show, filmed some sequences along with a Film Unit from the Central Office of Information and taken many photographs, but we needed more film and an opportunity to videotape a complete performance if we were to record sufficient for posterity.

When the invitation from the Nuffield Theatre Studio, University of Lancaster arrived, it seemed appropriate for possibly the oldest play in the world to go to one of the newest flexible theatres in the United Kingdom. Apart from the opportunity of presenting *The Triumph of Horus* again, it gave our students a unique opportunity.

Derek Poole was asked to direct the second production. He had reservations. The first production had been very demanding and had been compressed into a fortnight. Was it educationally sound to repeat a production instead of breaking new ground? Would students feel able to respond again to a formalised presentation that was in some ways the antithesis of work they were normally encouraged to do? The fourth-year student who had played the all-important Lector-

Priest had departed; so too had the fourth-year student who had sustained the demanding role of Isis; Thoth had gone, and some of the Chorus were not available, but above all this was a re-direction and whilst the first production had been satisfying it had seemed to Mr Poole that it pointed the way to a production that was more untrammelled, more clamorous and turbulent, more redolent of an age that combined high culture with violence and sacrifice, and this view he still holds. But the problems, inherent in mounting a different production were obviously at this time too great. Fortunately there were excellent cast replacements available; the studio at Lancaster would give us the space we had been short of at Padgate and, equally important, it would be possible to supplement the Crowd, which had been too small in the first production, and a crowd that could come nearer to having the effect of an Egyptian crowd of the period would add a different dimension to the production.

Several of the roles were re-cast, all successfully, and new Chorus members integrated perfectly with the help of the original players, but no major production alterations were made.

The Chorus space at Lancaster was slightly less than that used at Padgate, and was, in fact, in a 'pit' approximately five feet deep, so that the Chorus was below the seating level of the audience. This removed certain sight-line problems we had encountered but created others. Movement designed to be effective from the usual audience level had to be modified slightly because the audience would tend to be looking down on them, and the sight-lines from the audience edge of the pit meant that some sitting positions would be only half seen. Additionally, some seating half encircled the pit. Against these disadvantages was the great advantage of having much more space to work in on the stage proper. The set design for Lancaster was basically the same as for Padgate, but the stage units in use for supporting the platforms on which the Crowd played suggested a new idea, and the upstage ends of the diagonal walls were colonnaded, giving a varied and interesting background to the Chorus when it used the main stage.

Despite a steep ascent from pit to stage the Chorus performed very successfully, solving problems of changed timings on movements without much difficulty, and the Crowd, not perhaps as frenzied and unrestrained as the originals in Egypt must have been, nevertheless deepened and heightened the atmosphere impressively. Again one became aware that this was more than a religious ceremony. The Crowd, the original crowd, did not come to this ritual to watch, to stand outside the events, to sit apart; they came as participants, they came to join in the drama enacted, and this sense of participation came through to the students playing the parts of characters, Chorus, and Crowd at both Padgate and Lancaster. It enabled them to create an experience to which we sometimes give the name 'theatre', possibly meaning drama, which was originated by the text but which was dependent on a totality of involvement, so that the separate sections of players in performing their roles created an overall experience in which by 'doing', they became both creating performers and actual participants. It was not drama dependent on development of characters, or construction of plot, but on fundamentals of drama that underlie texts and are not really susceptible of literary criticism, though they are very powerful, owing more, perhaps, to magic than to rationalism.

But at the end it was Professor Fairman who indicated the underlying difficulty. He felt the second production had not only been worthwhile, but had added to the first, but, he said, there was 'Still not enough blood', and one wonders—or at least Mr Poole does—whether, despite the violence of the twentieth-century, our everyday lives are so genteel that there is a barrier to the full delineation of those characteristics of frenzy, abandon, even hysteria, which pervade this play and which are perhaps more familiar to us in works such as *The Bacchae*— and this despite Cup-ties and pop-star adulation.

How successful were we in bringing the play to life?

From our first radio version, then to the production at Padgate and the second version at Lancaster *we* were pleased. Pleased because we understood and pleased because we had gained in our own knowledge. Pleased because theatrical life had been given to a text that at one time had seemed beyond the bounds of our resources and imagination. Pleased because the opportunity could now be given for other groups of students and professional theatre companies to try their own approach.

Important was the fact that due to the chance of circumstances we were able to bring the play to the attention of a number of people interested in the roots of theatre development.

Responsible reporting of the production, in the press and on radio brought considerable interest from many parts of the world. One critic, Peter Fischer, in a broadcast to West Germany asked this question: 'How should one perform *The Triumph of Horus* today and how *did* Padgate College of Education perform it?' He went on,

> They had to rely on imaginative reconstruction, that has been a brilliant and wholly credible success. The Egyptian costumes, the animal masks and the colourful jewellery were all brilliant and were made by the students

themselves. The producer extended the use of colour by lighting and silhouette. These techniques were not of course used in front of the temple at Edfu, but they are a skilful compensation for the fact that a modern audience cannot possibly appreciate the many mythological allusions. The statuesque style of the production matches the strict stylised form of the text. Vitality and movement are provided by a chorus of young men and women who move between the temple walls. Appeals to the God are sometimes in a liturgical manner and accompanied by flutes and Egyptian percussion instruments. This choreographic style owes much to Greek models and perhaps this is correct, for since the Greeks knew of the Egyptian mystery plays, they in their turn may well have followed Egyptian models.

Anyway, one has the feeling that the 'Horus' play in Edfu might have been like this. What is was really like we shall never know. There are indeed many possibilities in the text. It is not simply an exercise in Egyptology. The theatre has been enriched by the resurrection of *The Triumph of Horus*.

What of the future? The dating of the play postulates interesting questions to theatre historians. For our students? They had an experience unique in drama training that should continue to develop throughout their careers.

We now have our videotape of *The Triumph of Horus* and a complete record, on tape, slide and film. Inevitably OUR next generation of students cannot share or recover that excitement that took place in our Drama Studio on the Sunday before production in June 1971 when the play came together for the first time in modern history. It has affected our thinking at Padgate College not only from the point of view of the roots of western theatre history but in our now being able to visualise concepts of the creative drama of earlier civilisations.

THE TRIUMPH OF HORUS

First presented on 23 June 1971 at the Padgate College of Education Drama Studio by the Department of Drama in Education and Theatre Crafts with the following cast:

Reader (Lector Priest)	Michael Jeffs
Horus, Lord of Behdet	Colin Angus
Horus, Lord of Mesen	Alan Murray
King	Rob Ellks
Queen	Elaine Kershaw
Isis	Helen Baron
Thoth	Martin Rayner
Chorus	Ian Booth, Christine Clifford, Richard Dann,

	Linda Easten, Jacqueline Ebbs, Mary Fairhurst, Diane Glasman, Heather Grimshaw, Sylvia Gomes, Mary Harding, Andreas Holland, Michael Langrish, Jennifer Lynch, Lynn Marshall, Christine Payton, Susan Pennell, Marion Wilson
Baboon Demon	Michael Robson
Bull Demon	Roger Wright
Lion Demon	Jeremy Mellonie
Servants to the Priest	Nigel Long, Stephen Minto, Alan Rabjohn
Young Harpooners	Maureen Berry, Gemma Carey, Linda Hilton, Ann Warnes
Upper Egyptian Princesses	Alison Davey, Gillian Frost, Ann Priestley, Carol Southall
Lower Egyptian Princesses	Janet Blane, Janet Crofts, Elizabeth Kent, Mary Stretton
Snake Dancer	Jacqueline Highton
Butcher	David J. Williams
Other parts played by	Gillian Argles, Joy Bett, Hilary Boyd, Jane

Butterworth, Jill Dobie, Anne Dobson, Monica Dove, Jennifer Fairman, Norma Fox, Katherine Guyton, Janet Heyes, William Hosker, Leslie Hosker, Sandra Jones, Patricia Mahoney, Janis Mailly, Barbara Mayne, Isabella O'Connor, Keith O'Mahoney, Beryl Rayner, Erika Rogers, Olwyn Sinclair, Wendy Turner, Michael Tyson

Second Production by the Padgate College of Education, Department of Drama in Education and Theatre Crafts, at the Nuffield Studio, University of Lancaster, 8 March 1972, with the following main changes in cast:

Reader	Nigel Long
Horus, Lord of Mesen	William Hammond
Queen	Lynn Marshall
Isis	Elaine Kershaw
Thoth	Gordon Aspden

Assistant Directors	Kathleen Brown, Jennifer Fairman, Laura Jefferies, William Hosker
Director (radio version)	Geoffrey Raymond
Director	June Fortune
General Director	Derek Poole
Producer	Derek Newton

THE
TRIUMPH OF
HORUS

Prologue

FIGURE 6   *In the background is the Pylon of the Temple of Edfu. In the
centre of the stage is a replica of the Sacred Lake of the temple and on it a boat.
The relief evidently depicts two phases in the development of the action.
First: to the right of the lake stand Thoth with the Reader (not depicted in the
relief) beside him. Beyond them are Horus the Behdetite, Horus Lord of Mesen
(not depicted in the relief), and Isis. To the left of the lake stand the King,
wearing the headdress of Onuris and holding a harpoon in his hand, and the
Queen (not depicted in the relief). The Reader holds a roll of papyrus from
which he reads. In the second phase, Horus the Behdetite, holding a rope in his
left hand and a harpoon in his right, and Isis will board the boat.*

CHORUS
   The King of Upper and Lower Egypt,
   Protector who protects his father,
   Great Warden who wards off the foe,
   It was he who established the sky upon its supports.
   Successful are all the things which he has done;   5
   Horus of the fierce countenance, who has slain the Caitiff,
   Horus the Behdetite, great god, lord of the sky.
READER
   Horus the Behdetite, great god, lord of the sky,
   Lord of Mesen, with dappled plumage, who came forth
                             from the horizon:

A hero of great strength when he sallied forth to battle　　　*10*
With his mother Isis protecting him

HORUS THE BEHDETITE

I cause Thy Majesty to prevail against him that is rebellious
　　　　　　　　　　　　　　　　　　　　toward thee
On the day of the melée.
I put valour and strength for thee into thy arms
And the might of my hands into thy hands.　　　*15*

READER

Isis the great, the god's mother,
Scorpion of Behdet, nurse of the Falcon of Gold.

ISIS

I give thee power against those who are hostile toward thee,
O my son Horus, thou lovable one.

READER

Horus Lord of Mesen, pre-eminent in Pe and Mesen,　　　*20*
Great God, pre-eminent in Wetjeset-Hor,
The Lion pre-eminent in Khant-Iabet,
Who drives Seth into the Wilderness,
Goodly Warden of the Two Lands and the River-banks,
Protector who protects Egypt.　　　*25*

HORUS LORD OF MESEN

I have come that I may slay the Hippopotamus with my weapons.
I guard Egypt from the Northerners,
A wall of brass around his Upper Egyptian Mesen,
Watchman over his Lower Egyptian Mesen.

READER

Thoth, twice great, lord of Hermopolis,　　　*30*
Him with the honeyed tongue, skilled in speech,
Who heralded the going of Horus to launch his war-galley,
Who overthrew his enemies with his utterances.

THOTH

A happy day for Horus, lord of this land,
Son of Isis, lovable one,　　　*35*
Winner of Triumph, offspring of Onnophris,
Whose strength is great in every place of his.

READER

The King of Upper and Lower Egypt, Heir-of-the-Beneficent-
　　Gods, Chosen-of-Ptah, Justiciar-of-Re, Living-Image-of-
　　Amun; Son of Re, Ptolemaeus-may-he-live-for-ever,
　　Beloved-of-Ptah;

Valiant in the fray, courageous with the thirty-barbed harpoon,
Who casts his weapon at his foes amain.   *40*
The Queen, the Mistress of the Two Lands, Cleopatra, God's
   Mother of the Son of Re, Ptolemaeus-may-he-live-for-ever-
   Beloved-of-Ptah.

CHORUS
   The King of Upper and Lower Egypt, a hero of great strength;
   Most warlike soul among the gods; who guards the Paths of
                                                Horus;
   Valorous one, of proud bearing
   When wielding the three-barbed harpoon; who travels swiftly
                                    in his war-galley;   *45*
   Lord of Mesen, captor of the Hippopotamus, who exercises
                                          protection.
   Horus the Behdetite, great god, lord of the sky.
   [*Horus the Behdetite, now equipped with a rope and a harpoon, and*
   Isis board the boat. Horus in the boat and the King upon land mime
   the harpooning of a hippopotamus]

READER
   Horus the Behdetite, great god, lord of the sky,
   Who on his father's behalf punished the Monster for what he
                                            had done,
   He turns himself about in his form of doughty harpooner   *50*
   And tramples on the backs of his foes.

HORUS THE BEHDETITE
   The single-barbed harpoon is in my left hand,
   The three-barbed in my grip,
   Let us slay yon Caitiff with our weapons.

READER
   Isis the great, the god's mother in Wetjeset-Hor,   *55*
   Who protects her son in his war-galley.

ISIS
   I fortify thy heart, my son Horus.
   Pierce thou the Hippopotamus, thy father's foe.

READER
   Long live the Good God, son of the Victorious Horus,
   Excellent offspring of the Lord of Mesen, bold fen-man,   *60*
   Valiant in the chase, the Prototype Man,
   Battling Horus, a man to seize the mooring-post in the water,
   Lord of Valour, Son of Re, Ptolemaeus-may-he-live-for-ever,
                                          Beloved-of-Ptah.

KING

Praise to thee and a merry noise to thy war-galley,
O Horus the Behdetite, great god, lord of the sky.   *65*
I adore thy name and the names of thy executioners in thy
                                                                  train.
I give praise to thy spearsmen,
I revere thy harpoons recorded in the ancient records,
I give thanks to thy weapons.

READER

Here begins the bringing to pass of the triumph of Horus   *70*
over his enemies when he hastened to slay the foes after the
sallying forth to battle. Seth has been judged in the
Tribunal of Re and Thoth says:—

THOTH

A happy day on this day which is divided by its minutes!
A happy day on this day which is divided by its hours!   *75*
A happy day in this month which is divided by its fifteenth-
                                                            day feast!
A happy day in this year which is divided by its months!
A happy day in this eternity which is divided by its years!
A happy day in this everlasting!
How pleasant it is when they come to thee every year!   *80*

HORUS THE BEHDETITE

A happy day! I have cast my harpoon lustily!
A happy day! My hands have the mastery of his head!
I have cast at the cows of the hippopotami in water of eight
                                                              cubits,
I have cast at the Lower Egyptian Bull in water of twenty
                                                              cubits,
A harpoon-blade of four cubits,   *85*
A rope of sixty cubits,
And a shaft of sixteen cubits being in my hands,
A stripling I of eight cubits.
I have cast standing in a war-galley on water of twenty
                                                              cubits.
I have hurled with my right hand,   *90*
And swung with my left,
As a bold fen-man does.

ISIS

The pregnant ones among the hippopotami give not birth,
Not one of their females conceives,

When they hear the thud of thy shaft 95
And the whistling of thy blade,
Like thunder in the east of heaven,
Like a drum in the hands of a child.
CHORUS AND ONLOOKERS
Hold fast, Horus, hold fast!

ACT I

The Harpoon Ritual · *Propitiating the God & His Weapons*

Scene i

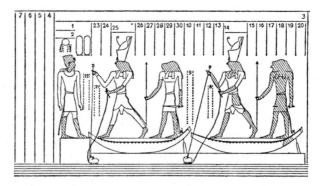

FIGURE 7   *The main setting is similar to that of the Prologue but two boats are on the Sacred Lake. In the first Horus Lord of Mesen accompanied by a baboon-headed demon and armed with harpoon and rope, thrusts his blade into the snout of a hippopotamus. In the second boat Horus the Behdetite, similarly armed and accompanied by another demon, pierces the head of a hippopotamus. Each demon carries a harpoon, blade uppermost, in his right hand and a knife in his left. On land stands the King facing the boat, his hands hanging down in an attitude of respect.*

CHORUS
    Praise to thee, praise to thy name,
    Horus the Behdetite, great god, lord of the sky,
    Goodly wall of copper round about Egypt.
DEMON
    I am Chief-of-the-Two-Lands-when-he-rises.
    I guard thee from him who is hostile to thee;   5
    I protect Thy Majesty with my charms.
    I rage against thy foes as a savage baboon.
    I lay low thine enemies in thy path.
    I am the Guard of Thy Majesty every day

I protect Thy Majesty every day.   10
I am the first demon of thy crew.

KING

The first of the weapons which rushed after him who
                                           assailed Horus
And took the breath from the snout of the Hippopotamus.

HORUS LORD OF MESEN

The first harpoon is stuck fast in his snout and has severed
                                           his nostrils.
The blade takes hold in the head of the Hippopotamus in the
                                  Place of Confidence.   15

CHORUS

O Horus, fair are thy trappings of giraffe's hair,
Thy net which is Min's,
And thy shaft which belongs to the spear of Onuris.
Thy arm was the first to cast the harpoon.
Those upon the banks rejoice at the sight of thee,   20
As at the rising of Sothis at the year's beginning,
When they behold thy weapons raining down in mid-stream
Like the moon-beams when the sky is peaceful.
Horus is in his bark like Wenty,
Having overthrown the hippopotami from his war-galley.   25

CHORUS AND ONLOOKERS

Hold fast, Horus, hold fast!

DEMON

I am Offerer-who-apportions-his-offerings.
I am with thee in the melée
That I may punish the transgressions of thine enemy.
I break his bones, I smash his vertebrae,   30
I crunch his flesh, I swallow his gore.

KING

Thy lance which brought in the Caitiff though he was afar;
It has cleft the crown of the head of the Hippopotamus.

HORUS THE BEHDETITE

The second harpoon is stuck fast in his forehead;
It has cleft the crown of the head of the enemy.   35

CHORUS

Grasp firmly the harpoon, breathe the air in Khemmis,
O Lord of Mesen,
Captor of the Hippopotamus, Creator of Joy,
Goodly Falcon who boards his boat

And takes to the river in his war-galley; 40
Prototype Man, Battling Horus!
Those who are in the water are afraid of him,
Awe of him fills those who are on the bank.
Thou subjugator of every one,
Thou whose thews are strong, 45
The Perverse One in the water fears thee.
Thou smitest and woundest as if it were Horus who cast the
harpoon,
Even the Victorious Bull, Lord of Prowess.
The Son of Re has done for Horus even as Horus himself did,
Yea, the Son of Re has done likewise. 50
Let thy talons grip the second harpoon.

CHORUS AND ONLOOKERS

Hold fast, Horus, hold fast!

Scene ii

FIGURE 8 *The setting is similar to that of Scene i. In the first boat, Horus Lord of Mesen armed with harpoon and rope, pierces the neck of a hippopotamus. In the second, Horus the Behdetite, similarly armed, plunges a harpoon into the head of a hippopotamus. In each boat is also a bull-headed demon, armed as in Scene i. On land, the King stands facing the boats, with his hands raised in adoration.*

CHORUS
    Praise to thee, Horus the Behdetite, great god, lord of the
                                        sky,
    Wall of stone round about Egypt,
    Excellent protector, guardian of the temples,
    Who drives back the Perverse One from the Two Outpourings,
    The goodly Watchman of the Fortress.   5
DEMON
    I am Bull-of-the-Two-Lands.
    I assault him who comes to profane thy palace;
    I gore with my horns him who plots against it.
    Blood on my horns and dust behind me
    For every violator of thy nome.   10
KING
    Make a slaughtering! Let its barb bite into the neck of the
                              Hippopotamus!
HORUS LORD OF MESEN
    The third harpoon is stuck fast in his neck,
    Its barbs, they bite into his flesh.

CHORUS
> Hail to thee, the one that sleeps alone,
> That communes with his own heart only, 15
> A man to seize the mooring-post in the water.

ISIS
> Cast thy harpoon, I pray thee,
> At the mound of the Savage Beast.
> See, thou art on a mound clear of bushes,
> A shore free from scrub. 20
> Fear not his awfulness;
> Flee not because of them that are in the water.
> Let thy harpoon fasten on to him,
> My son Horus.

READER
> Isis, she says to Horus: 25

ISIS
> Thy foes are fallen beneath thee,
> So eat thou the flesh of the neck,
> The abomination of women.
> The noise of lamentation is in the southern sky,
> Wailing is in the northern sky, 30
> The noise of the lamentation of my brother Seth.
> My son Horus has him fast holden.

CHORUS AND ONLOOKERS
> Hold fast, Horus, hold fast!

DEMON
> I am Black Bull.
> I eat the flesh, I swallow the gore, 35
> Of them that cause alarm in thy temple.
> I turn my face toward him who comes against thy house,
> I drive away the Caitiff from the temples.

KING
> My horn gores the Marauder when he shows himself.
> It has sundered the vessels in the head of the Hippopotamus. 40

HORUS THE BEHDETITE
> The fourth harpoon is stuck fast in his pate;
> It has cut open the vessels of his head, the back parts in
> > his head.

CHORUS
> Grasp the harpoon which Ptah, the goodly guide, fashioned
> > for the Fen-goddess,

Which was fashioned in copper for thy mother Isis.

ISIS

I have made raiment for the Fen-goddess,   *45*
For the Goddess of Weaving,
For the Nurse, for Sothis,
For the Goddess of Raiment
And for the Lady of the Chase.
Be firm on thy feet against yon Hippopotamus,   *50*
Hold him fast with thy hand.

HORUS THE BEHDETITE

I have cast my harpoon at the Lower Egyptian Bull,
I have sore wounded Terrible Face,
I plough up the river with my weapons from upon the bank
I reach the water and approach the river.   *55*

ISIS

Let thy harpoon fasten on to him, my son Horus,
On to yon enemy of thy father.
Drive thy blade into him, my son Horus,
That thy shaft may bite into his skin.
Let thy hands drag yon Caitiff.   *60*

CHORUS AND ONLOOKERS

Hold fast, Horus, hold fast!

Scene iii

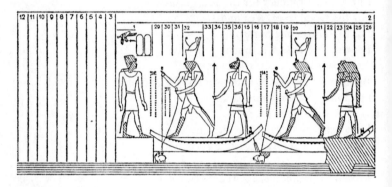

FIGURE 9 *The setting is similar to that of Scenes i and ii. Horus Lord of Mesen and Horus the Behdetite pierce a hippopotamus in the flank and back. The attendant demons are lion-headed. The King stands on land, facing the boats, in the same attitude as in Scene i.*

CHORUS
    We praise thy face, thou valiant harpooner,
    O Horus the Behdetite, great god, lord of the sky,
    Adoring thy image,
    Making obeisance to thy form,
    Worshipping thine ancestors.   5
    We grant strength to thine arm
    That thy Majesty may prevail over thy foes.
    Thy Majesty placeth them as a protection round about Mesen,
    Unendingly and unceasingly forever.

DEMON
    I am Shining Bull.   10
    I cut out the hearts of those who fight against thy city of
                                Behdet.
    I tear out the hearts of thy foes,
    I swallow the gore of those who are hostile to thy city,
    I taste the kidneys of thine enemies.

KING
    The first arrow which has no rival, the fifth of the weapons,   15
    It has cleft open the ribs of the Lower Egyptian Bull.

HORUS LORD OF MESEN
The fifth harpoon is stuck fast in his flank,
It has cleft open his ribs.

CHORUS
Thrust home the harpoon; spread wide the rope;
Make common cause with Horus, who shoots amain.　　　20
Lo, thou art a Nubian in Khent-hen-nufer,
Yet thou dwellest in a temple,
For Re has given thee his kingship
With the intent to overthrow the Hippopotamus.

ISIS
The cry of the Hippopotamus fallen in thy rope!　　　25
Alack, alack in Khargeh!
The boat is light and he who is in it is a child,
Yet yon Caitiff who is in thy rope is fallen.

CHORUS AND ONLOOKERS
Hold fast, Horus, hold fast!

DEMON
I am He-loves-Solitude.　　　30
I sharpen my teeth in order to bite thy foes.
I whet my talons to seize hold of their skins.

KING
The sixth harpoon, which devours everyone who
　　　　　　　　　　　　　　　　confronts it.
It has sundered the vertebrae of the backs of thy foes.

HORUS THE BEHDETITE
The sixth harpoon is stuck fast in his ribs,　　　35
It has sundered his vertebrae.

READER
I wash my mouth, I chew natron,
That I may extol the might of Horus son of Isis,
The goodly stripling who came forth from Isis,
Son of Osiris, the lovable one.　　　40
Horus has hurled his harpoon with his hand,
He whose arm was strong from the first,
When he established the sky upon its four supports.
Successful are the deeds which he has done.

CHORUS
Lo, Busiris, Mendes, Heliopolis,　　　45
Letopolis, Pe, Dep, Memphis,
Hermopolis, Hebenu, the Oryx Nome,

The Nome of Him-with-the-outspread-talons, He-nesu
                                    Heracleopolis,
Abydos, Panopolis, Coptos, Assiut,
Behdet, Mesen and Denderah are in joy,   50
Making jubilation when they see
This beauteous and enduring memorial
Which Horus son of Isis has made.
He has built the Throne, adorned with gold,
Overlaid and finished with electrum.   55
Its sanctuary is beautiful and noble,
Like unto the seat of the Master of the Universe,
His Majesty dwells in Memphis,
The Coasts of Horus adoring him, on the estate of his father
                                    Osiris.

READER
He has taken the office of his father,   60
Winning him triumph and avenging him.
FEMALE CHORUS
Seth thought to oppress him
MALE CHORUS
But Horus attacked him.
READER
How pleasant is the father's kingly office,
To his son who has vindicated him.   65
He gives thanks for it.
ISIS
Thou who didst act under my guidance,
Thou hast dealt with the malady.
Thou hast oppressed him who oppressed thee.
My son Horus has grown up in his strength   70
And was from the first ordained to avenge his father.
READER
The sky was cleared for him by the north wind,
The Two Lands were strewn with Upper Egyptian emeralds,
Because Horus had built his war galley
In order to go therein to the fen   75
To overthrow the enemies of his father Osiris,
To seize for him the disaffected.
HORUS THE BEHDETITE
I am Horus, son of Osiris,
Who smote the foes and overthrew his enemies.

ISIS

How pleasant is it to walk along the shore unhindered,   *80*
To pass through the water without the sand swelling up
                                           under thy feet,
And no thorn pricks them, the crocodiles are not uncovered,
Thy grandeur having been seen and thy shaft planted in them,
My son Horus.

CHORUS AND ONLOOKERS

Hold fast, Horus, hold fast!   *85*

Scene iv

FIGURE 10   *The setting is similar to that of the previous scenes. Two boats
are on the Sacred Lake: in one Horus Lord of Mesen drives his harpoon into the
testicles of a hippopotamus, which is lying on its back, legs in the air; in the
other boat, Horus the Behdetite pierces the hindquarters of a hippopotamus.
The demons, armed as before, are lion-headed. The King stands
on the shore with hands raised in adoration.*

CHORUS
   Praise to thy face, glory to thy might,
   O Horus the Behdetite, great god, lord of the sky,
   Strong wall, warlike falcon,
   Excelling in strength, greatly feared,
   Who wounds him who seeks his hurt;   5
   A hero of great strength, whose boundary cannot be
                                    overthrown;
   Leader of his company to repel Be,
   Protector of the Mansion of the Falcon; sharp of talons;
   Ferocious One who guards Mesen unceasingly and
                             unremittingly.
   Thy valour and thy might are round about thy temple   *10*
   For the length of eternity.
DEMON
   I am His-Speech-is-Fire.
   I make ruby-red my eyes and blood-red my eye-balls.
   I repel those who come with evil intent toward thy seat.
   I eat their flesh, I swallow their gore,   *15*
   I burn their bones with fire.

KING

The seventh harpoon which cleaves to his body,
Which has mangled his limbs and skewered the Hippopotamus
From his belly to his testicles.

HORUS LORD OF MESEN

The seventh harpoon is stuck fast in his body,   20
It has spiked his testicles.

READER

Isis uttered a cry, speaking to the fatherless child battling
    with Pnehes.

ISIS

Be of good courage, Horus my son.
Lo, thou hast him fast holden, yon enemy of thy father.   25
Be not wearied because of him.
One hand grapples with thy harpoon in his hide,
Two hands grapple with thy rope.
Thy blade, it has bitten into his bones,
I have seen thy blade in his belly.   30
Thy horn playing havoc with his bones.

CHORUS

Ye who are in heaven and earth, fear Horus!
Ye who are in the abyss, do him reverence!
Lo, he has appeared in glory as a mighty king,
He has taken the throne of his father.   35
The right arm of Horus is as those of the young fen-men.
Eat ye the flesh of the foe,
Drink ye of his gore;
Swallow them up,
Ye who are in the abyss.   40

INTERLUDE

READER

Letopolis. The slaying of *sabet*-snakes for his mother Isis.
(*The action of Scene iv is interrupted at this point by a brief
Interlude in which the mythological cutting off of the heads of the
enemies of Horus is mimed. The heads of the snakes are cut off
and there is a ritual eating and drinking of their flesh and blood.
Immediately afterwards the action continues. The words assigned
here to the Reader are in reality a Stage Direction.*)

READER

    Isis came, having found the Hippopotamus standing with
    feet on dry land. Water was created between his fighting-
    place and her son Horus. She says:

ISIS

    Lo, I am come as the Mother from Khemmis   45
    That I may make an end for thee of the Hippopotamus
    Which has crushed the nest of my chick
    The boat is light, and he who is in it is but a child,
    Yet yon Caitiff who is in thy rope is fallen.

CHORUS AND ONLOOKERS

    Hold fast, Horus, hold fast!   50

DEMON

    I am He-who-comes-forth-with-Mouth-aflame.
    I quell the assailant of the Balcony of the Falcon.
    I, as an ape, turn back him who is hostile toward it.

KING

    Adoration of the raging sacred harpoon which stirs up
                    confusion.
    The eighth harpoon, it has laid hold on the hind quarters of
                    thy foe,   55
    It has ripped open his haunches.

HORUS THE BEHDETITE

    The eighth harpoon is stuck fast in his hind quarters,
    It has ripped up his haunches.

READER

    Let thy divine harpoon bite into his face
    O Horus, be not troubled because of him.   60
    Onuris is the protector of thy rending talons;
    The *deses*-fish shall not bite in the turmoil.
    How many dost thou spike when thy talons take hold,
    When thy shaft has been made ready in thy hand!
    Thou cuttest up the flesh in the morning.   65
    Thy arrows are those of the Master of the Bird-pool.
    Satisfaction of thy throat is given thee,
    So say the young craftsmen.
    It is Ptah who presents it to thee.

CHORUS

    Hail Horus, beloved of the young fen-men!   70
    Lo, thou art a diving bird which transfixes the fish in the
                    water.

Lo, thou art an ichneumon, firmly poised upon its claws,
which seizes the prey with its paw.
Lo, thou art a hunter's hound which breaketh through the fat
of the neck in order to eat the flesh.
Lo, thou art a stripling of sturdy build, who slays one
mightier than himself.
Lo, thou art a fierce lion, ready for the fray upon the
river-bank, which standeth astride the carcass.   75
Lo, thou art a flame, well-kindled, inspiring fear, which rages
on a hillock of brushwood.

CHORUS AND ONLOOKERS
Hold fast, Horus, hold fast!

Scene v

FIGURE II *Setting is basically unchanged. In the first boat Horus Lord of Mesen thrusts his harpoon into the hindquarters of a hippopotamus which is standing upright. In the other boat Horus the Behdetite harpoons the feet of a hippopotamus which is lying on its back. The demons are lion-headed and armed in the usual way. The King stands on the shore in the same attitude as in Scenes i and iii.*

READER
Adoration of the sacred harpoon.

CHORUS
Glory be to thy spirit, thou spearsman of great strength,
Horus the Behdetite, great god, lord of the sky.
Adoration to thy avenging angels, thy followers,
Thy messengers and thy watchmen who watch over thy
sanctuary.   5
Glory be to thy war-galley, thy mother,
Thy nurse, who dandled thy loveliness upon her knees.
Praise be to thy blade, thy shaft,
Thy ropes and this thy armoury for overthrowing thy foes.
Thy Majesty setteth them for a protection round about thy
temple.   10
Thy spirit safeguardeth Mesen for ever.

DEMON
I am Death-in-his-Face-Loud-Screamer.
I encompass Thy Majesty about as a wall,
A palisade protecting thy spirit on the day of conflict.

I watch over thy temple by day and by night,   *15*
Warding off the foe from thy shrine.

HORUS LORD OF MESEN
The ninth harpoon is stuck fast in his legs,
Entering the flesh of the hippopotamus.

CHORUS
Let thy harpoon lay hold on him, Horus, fierce of face,
Alert son of the Master of the Universe.   *20*
At dawn thy wonders are seen
Like those of Haroeris, on the river-banks.
Can it be that a brother hates his brother who is older
than he?
Who will love him?
He will fall by the rope of Shesmu,   *25*
As spoil of the Lady of the Chase.

ISIS
Hast thou called to mind how when we were in Lower Egypt
The Father of the Gods sent us the gods to row us,
Sopd being our helmsman?
How the gods were united in watching over us,   *30*
Each one of them skilled in his trade?
How Khentekhtai steered us,
And Geb showed us the way.

CHORUS AND ONLOOKERS
Hold fast, Horus, hold fast!

DEMON
I am Fiery-Face-who-brings-in-the-Mutilated-One.   *35*
I drink the blood of him who would overthrow thy sanctuary,
I cut in pieces the flesh of him who would violate thy
shrine.
I give thee the valour and might of my arms
And the strength of My Majesty against thine enemies.

HORUS THE BEHDETITE
The tenth harpoon is stuck fast in his hocks.   *40*

THE YOUNG HARPOONERS
Come and cause him to subjugate him who would make him
submissive.

CHORUS
Seize ye and lay hold, ye lords of strength;
Plunder, ye masters of savage beasts!
Drink ye the blood of your foes and of their females;

Sharpen your knives, whet your blades,   45
Steep your weapons in the blood!
Yours are the bodies of lions in the hidden covert.
Yours are the bodies of hippopotami, whose abomination is
                                                  mildness.
Yours are the bodies of geese which run along the shore,
Their hearts elated at alighting thereon.   50
CHORUS AND ONLOOKERS
    Hold fast, Horus hold fast!

ACT II

The Rejoicing over the the Victory

Scene i

FIGURE 12   *The Sacred Lake, in the background the pylon of the temple. On
the lake, a large ship, its sail distended by the wind. In the middle of the boat
stands Horus: with his right hand he thrusts his harpoon into the snout of a
hippopotamus; he holds in his left hand two ropes attached to two harpoons
already lodged in the body of the animal. Isis squats in the bows and holds two
similar ropes. On shore, facing the ship, the King stands and thrusts a harpoon
into the back of the head of the hippopotamus.*

CHORUS
    Come, let us hasten to the Pool of Horus,
    That we may see the Falcon in his ship,
    That we may see the Son of Isis in his war-galley,
    Like Re in the Bark of the Morning.
    His harpoon is held firmly in his grip   5
    As in that of Horus of the Mighty Arm.
    He casts and drags
    That he may bring captive the Hippopotamus
    And slay the Lower Egyptian Bull.
    Rejoice, ye inhabitants of Retribution-Town!   *10*

Alack, alack in Khargeh!

HORUS

I hold fast, pilot in my war-galley.
I hurl my thirty-barbed harpoon at the snout of the
                                        hippopotamus,
While my mother Isis protects me.

KING

The harpooner am I, of upright carriage, when wielding the
                                three-barbed-harpoon.   *15*

CHORUS

Seize thy baldric!
Come down and stand fast,
Having thy adornments which belong to Hedjhotpe,
Thy net which belongs to Min,
Which was woven for thee and spun for thee   *20*
By Hathor, Mistress of the Coriander.
A meal of forelegs is assigned thee
And thou eatest it eagerly.
The gods of the sky are in terror of Horus.
Hear ye the cries of Nehes!   *25*
Steady Horus!
Flee not because of them that are in the water;
Fear not them that are in the stream.
Hearken not when he pleads with thee.

CHORUS AND ONLOOKERS

Hold fast, Horus, hold fast!   *30*

ISIS

Take to thy war-galley, my son Horus whom I love,
The nurse who dandles Horus upon the water,
Hiding him beneath her timbers,
The deep gloom of the pines.
There is no fear when backing to moor,   *35*
For the goodly rudder turns on its post
Like Horus on the lap of his mother Isis.
The strakes are fixed upon the ribs,
Like the vizier in the palace.
The mast stands firmly on the footstep,   *40*
Like Horus when he became ruler over this land.
That beauteous sail of dazzling brightness
Is like Nut the Great when she was pregnant with the gods.
The two lifts, one is Isis, the other Nephthys,

Each of them firmly holding what appertains to them upon
                                        the yard-arms,   *45*
Like brothers of one mother mated in wedlock.
The rowlocks are fixed upon the gunwale,
Like the ornaments of princes.
The oars beat on either side of her,
Like heralds when they proclaim the joust.   *50*
The planks adhere closely together
And are not parted the one from the other.
The deck is like a writing-board filled with the images of
                                        goddesses.
The baulks in the hold are like pillars standing firmly in
                                        a temple
The belaying-pins in the bulwarks are like a noble snake
                                whose back is concealed.   *55*
The scoop of real lapis-lazuli bales out the water as fine
                                        unguent,
While the weed scurries in front of her like a great snake
                                        into its hole.
The hawser is beside the post like a chick beside its mother.
CHORUS AND ONLOOKERS
    Hold fast, Horus, hold fast!
    (*Enter the Young Harpooners at a run, each carrying a harpoon
    and a dagger*)
THE YOUNG HARPOONERS
    We are the royal children and crew of Horus,   *60*
    The Harpooners of the Lord of Mesen,
    The valorous Harpooners of Horus the Behdetite,
    Who thrust to make an end of his enemies,
    Adepts at holding fast,
    Stalwart heroes, whose weapons reach the mark,   *65*
    Who pierce the deep water,
    Whose shafts flash behind the robber-beasts,
    Whose blades seize on their flesh,
    Whose arms are strong when dragging the foes.
    They reach Mesen rejoicing greatly.   *70*
READER
    Isis said to the Young Harpooners when she saw their
        shapely hands:
ISIS
    Assault ye the foe!

Slay ye him in his lair!
Slaughter ye him in his destined moment here and now! 75
Plunge your knives into him again and again!
The gods of the sky are in terror of Horus.
Hear ye the cry of Nehes.
Steady Horus!
Flee not because of them that are in the water! 80
Fear not them that are in the stream!
Hearken not when he pleads with thee,
When he is fast holden in thy grasp, my son Horus.
Lay hold, Horus, lay hold on the harpoon-shaft
I, yea, I, am the lady of the shaft. 85
I am the beautiful one, the mistress of the loud-screamer,
When it comes forth upon the banks
And gleams after the robber-beast,
Which rips open his skin,
And breaks open his ribs 90
When the barbs enter his belly.
I forget not the night of the flood,
The hour of turmoil.

CHORUS AND ONLOOKERS
Hold fast, Horus, hold fast.

Scene ii

FIGURE 13   *The Sacred Lake, before the Pylons. This relief is to be
interpreted as a double one, depicting successive moments in the triumph and
coronation of Horus. The King is not depicted nor is any speaking part
assigned to him. This is because the King is now the Living Horus on earth,
the triumph of Horus is his triumph, the coronation of Horus is his coronation.
First, extreme right of the relief, Horus stands on land and, as an epitome of all
that has previously happened and as a justification of the ensuing coronation,
mimes the killing of the hippopotamus. He then boards his sacred bark,
followed by Thoth who invests him with the insignia of kingship and finally
crowns him. The Queen stands beside the lake and rattles a pair of sistra. On
either side of the lake, facing each other, are two groups of women with
tambourines in their hands: they represent the Lower Egyptian Princesses (lower
group) and the Upper Egyptian Princesses (upper group) and sing antiphonically
a hymn of praise and triumph. In accordance with protocol and their position
on the relief, the Lower Egyptian Princesses sing the first stanza.*

CHORUS

How happy is thy countenance, now that thou hast appeared
gloriously in thy bark,
O Horus the Behdetite, great god, lord of the sky,
Like Re in the Bark of the Morning,
When thou hast received thine office with crook and flail,
And art crowned with the Double Diadem of Horus,   5
Sekhmet prevailing over him that is rebellious toward thee,
Thoth the Great protecting thee.
Thine inheritance is thine, great god, son of Osiris,

Now that thou hast smitten the Lower Egyptian Bull.
Be glad of heart, ye inhabitants of the Great Seat,　　　　　*10*
Horus has taken possession of the throne of his father.

CHORUS AND ONLOOKERS
Horus has taken possession of the throne of his father.

HORUS
I am Horus the Behdetite, great god, lord of the sky, lord
　　　　　　　　　　　　　　　　　　of Mesen;
Wenty who pierces the Unsuccessful One, his foe;
Him-with-the-Upraised-Arm who wields the three-barbed
　　　　　　harpoon in order to slay his enemies.　　　*15*
(*Horus thrusts his harpoon into the head of the hippopotamus*)
I cast my thirty-barbed harpoon at the snout of the
　　　　　　　　　　　　　　　　　Hippopotamus,
I wound the foeman of Him-who-is-on-the-Mound.
(*Horus embarks on the boat and seats himself on a throne. Thoth
takes position behind.*)

HORUS
I am Horus the Behdetite, great god, lord of the sky,
Lord of the Upper Egyptian crown,
Prince of the Lower Egyptian crown,　　　　　*20*
King of the Kings of Upper Egypt,
King of the Kings of Lower Egypt,
Beneficent Prince, the Prince of princes.
I receive the crook and the whip,
(*Horus is given the crook and flail*)
For I am the lord of this land.　　　　　*25*
I take possession of the Two Lands
In assuming the Double Diadem.
(*Horus is crowned with the double crown*)
I overthrow the foe of my father Osiris
As King of Upper and Lower Egypt for ever.

CHORUS AND ONLOOKERS
King of Upper and Lower Egypt for ever!　　　　　*30*

THOTH
I overthrow thy enemies,
I protect thy bark with my potent spells.

QUEEN
I make music for thy pleasure,
O thou who shinest as King of Upper and Lower Egypt,
Thine enemies being in hordes beneath thee.　　　　　*35*

106

READER

The Lower Egyptian princesses and the women of Busiris
  rejoice over Horus at his victory.

LOWER EGYPTIAN PRINCESSES

We rejoice over thee, we delight in beholding thee,
We exult at the sight of thy fair face.

READER

The Upper Egyptian princesses and the women of Pe   40
  and Dep rejoice over Horus at his appearance in glory.

UPPER EGYPTIAN PRINCESSES

We rejoice over thee, we are gladdened by the sight of thee
When thou arisest in brightness for us as King of Upper and
                                        Lower Egypt.

LOWER EGYPTIAN PRINCESSES

We raise thee joyful praise to the height of heaven,
When thou punishest the misdeeds of thine enemy.   45

UPPER EGYPTIAN PRINCESSES

We beat the tambourine for thee, we exult at seeing thee,
When thou receivest the office of Harakhte.

LOWER EGYPTIAN PRINCESSES

We worship thee and hymn Thy Majesty,
For thou hast laid low the enemy of thy father.

UPPER EGYPTIAN PRINCESSES

We make jubilation to thy similitude,   50
When thou shinest for us like Re shining in the horizon.

QUEEN

Rejoice, ye women of Busiris and ye townsfolk beside Andjet.
Come and see Horus, who has pierced the Lower Egyptian Bull!
He wallows in the blood of the foe,
  His harpoon-shaft achieving a swift capture.   55
He makes the river to flow, blood-stained,
Like Sekhmet in a blighted year.

WOMEN OF BUSIRIS

Thy weapons plunge in mid-stream
Like a wild goose beside her young ones.

CHORUS AND ONLOOKERS

Hold fast, Horus, hold fast!   60

QUEEN

Rejoice, ye women of Pe and Dep, ye townsfolk beside the
                                        marshes!
Come and see Horus in the prow of his ship,

Like Re when he shines in the horizon,
Arrayed in green cloth, clad in red cloth,
Decked in his ornaments,   *65*
The White Crown and the Red Crown firmly set on his head,
The two uraei between his brows.
He has received the crook and the whip,
Being crowned with Double Diadem,
While Sekhmet abides in front of him   *70*
And Thoth protects him.

WOMEN OF PE AND DEP
It is Ptah who has shaped thy shaft,
Sokar who has forged thy weapons.
It is Hedjhotpe in the Beauteous Place who has made thy
                                             rope from yarn.
Thy harpoon-blade is of sheet-copper,   *75*
Thy shaft of zizyphus-wood from abroad.

HORUS
I have hurled with my right hand,
I have swung with my left hand,
As does a bold fen-man.

CHORUS AND ONLOOKERS
Hold fast, Horus, hold fast!   *80*

ACT III

The Celebration of the Victory

Scene i

THE FIRST DISMEMBERMENT OF SETH

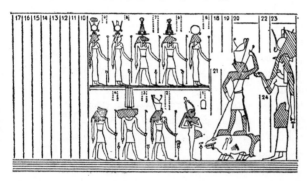

FIGURE 14 *Horus the Behdetite stands on the back of a hippopotamus, whose head he pierces with his harpoon. Facing him are nine gods: an offering stand, empty, is in front of each divinity. Isis stands behind Horus, supporting his upraised left arm with her right hand.*

ISIS
> Be glad of heart, my son Horus.
> Thine enemy has fallen and is not.

HORUS
> Raise thyself up. Osiris, great god, ruler of eternity.
> He who was hostile to thee is dismembered.

READER
> Isis opened her mouth to speak to her son Horus, Saying: 5

ISIS
> If thou cuttest up thy great Hippopotamus, hasten thou to me
>   and draw nigh me that I may instruct thee.
> (*Horus descends from the hippopotamus and begins to cut it up as
> Isis speaks. The various portions are carried to the appropriate
> gods and placed on the offering stand before each.*)

ISIS

I say unto thee:
Let his foreleg be taken to Busiris, for thy father Osiris-
                              Onnophris the triumphant.
Consign his ribs to Iyet for Haroeris pre-eminent in
                              Letopolis,   10
While his shank remains in This for thy great father Onuris.
Consign his shoulder to Yebt for thy great brother
                              Wepwawet.
Consign his breast to Assiut for Tefnut mistress of Medjed.
Give his thigh to Khnum-Haroeris, him whose feats are many,
    great god, lord of the knife, lord of strength, who overthrows
    the foes, for he is thy great brother.   15
Give the large meat-portion of him to Khnum, lord of
    Elephantine, great god, Lord of the Cataract, that he may
    increase the crew of thy war-galley.
Give his rump to Nephthys, for she is thy great sister.
Mine is his forepart, mine is his hinderpart, for I am she
    who rescued the heart of the Weary-Hearted One, him
    whose heart failed.
Give his bones to the cats,
His fat to the worms,   20
His suet to the Young Harpooners, that they may know the
                              taste of his flesh,
Give the whole forepart to their children, that they may
                              perceive the sweetness of his form,
And the choice portion of his limbs to thy followers, that
                              they may savour the taste of his flesh.
So shall they drive thy harpoon deep within him my son
                              Horus,
Even the holy harpoon that has entered into him, that
                              enemy of thy father Osiris.   25

CHORUS AND ONLOOKERS
Hold fast, Horus, hold fast!

Scene ii

FIGURE 15

CHORUS
    The noise of rejoicing resounds in Mesen;
    Gladness issues from Behdet.
    Horus has come that he may slay the Nubian
    And his confederates in the place of slaughter.
    He has cut off his head,   5
    He has cut out his heart,
    He has drenched him in his own blood.
    Wetjeset-Hor and Denderah are in jubilation.
    Alack, alack in Kenset!

ISIS
    Behold, I am come as the Mother from Khemmis   10
    That I may make an end for thee of the Hippopotamus.
    Pray be strong, thou fierce lion.
    Stand firm on thy feet against yon Hippopotamus
    And hold him fast.
    (*In dumb show Horus thrusts a harpoon into the back of a*
    small model of a hippopotamus. Simultaneously, the King
    who is facing Horus, harpoons the buttocks of a somewhat
    larger figure of a bound human captive)

KING
    Horus has come that he may carry off the Hippopotamus   15
    To his Residence in Pe and Mesen.

Rejoice, O ye of Retribution-Town,
Horus has overthrown his enemies.
Be glad, ye citizens of Denderah,
Horus has stabbed him that was disloyal to him   *20*
And he no longer exists.

Scene iii

THE SECOND DISMEMBERMENT OF SETH

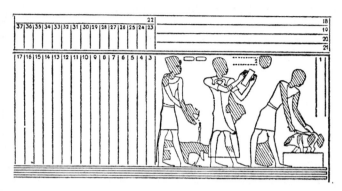

FIGURE 16   *A butcher cuts up with a knife a model hippopotamus made of cake.
The Lector, impersonating Imhotep, wears a leopard skin vestment over a long
linen robe and recites from a roll of papyrus held in his hands. The King
pours grain from a cup into the open beak of a goose.*

ISIS

> Thou seizest thy harpoon and doest what thou wilt with it,
> My son Horus, thou lovable one.

READER

> The King of Upper and Lower Egypt, Heir-of-the-
>   Beneficent-Gods, Chosen-of-Ptah, Justiciar-of-Re, Living-
>   Image-of-Amun; the Son of Re, Lord of Diadems,
>   Ptolemaeus-may-he-live-forever, Beloved-of-Ptah, is
>   triumphant in the Broad Hall.
> He has overthrown the Beduin of all the countries of Asia.
> Lo, he is triumphant in the Broad Hall,   5
> He has suppressed his enemies,
> He has taken hold of their backs,
> He has clutched the foe by their forelocks.
> Bring in the hippopotamus in the form of a cake into the
>   presence of Him-with-the-Upraised-Arm.   10
> (*A cake shaped like a hippopotamus is brought in. The Butcher
> enters*)

BUTCHER

> I am the skilled butcher of the Majesty of Re,

113

Who cuts up the Hippopotamus, dismembered upon his hide.
READER
    Dismembering by the Butcher. Recitation of this book
       against Seth by the Chief Lector Priest on the twenty-
       first day of the second month of Winter.   15
    (*As the Butcher cuts up the cake, the Reader recites from the
    papyrus roll held in his hands*)
READER
    Be thou annihilated, O Seth, be thou annihilated!
    Thou shalt not exist and thy soul shall not exist.
    Thou shalt not exist and thy body shall not exist.
    Thou shalt not exist and thy children shall not exist.
    Thou shalt not exist and thy flesh shall not exist.   20
    Thou shalt not exist and thy bones shall not exist.
    Thou shalt not exist and thy magic shall not exist.
    Thou shalt not exist and no place where thou art shall exist.
    Thou shalt die,
CHORUS
    die!   25
READER
    Mayest thou perish, may thy name perish.
    Fall upon thy face.
    Be felled,
CHORUS
    felled!
READER
    Be crushed,   30
CHORUS
    crushed!
READER
    Be annihilated,
CHORUS
    annihilated!
READER
    Be cut to pieces,
CHORUS
    to pieces!   35
READER
    Be cut up,
CHORUS
    cut up!

READER
The barb of Horus is thrust into thy brow;
Thy head is severed from thy neck;
Thou art destroyed at the execution-block;   40
Thy head is cut off and thou art cast on thy back.
The prophets, fathers of the god and priests say:
PROPHETS, FATHERS OF THE GOD AND PRIESTS
Be glad, ye women of Busiris:
Horus has overthrown his enemies.
Rejoice, ye women of Wetjeset-Hor: 45
Horus the Behdetite, great god, lord of the sky, has over-
                          thrown yon foe of his father Osiris.
O Onnophris, thy strength is restored to thee;
They who are in the abyss fear thee;
The lords of the thrones shout in joy to thee.
CHORUS
This is Horus, the protector of his father Osiris,   50
Who fights with his horns,
Who prevails over the Hippopotamus,
Who seizes the Perverse One,
Who smites the foes.
READER
Bring in the goose and let grain be poured into its mouth.   55
(*A goose and a cup of grain are brought in. The King pours the
grain into the mouth of the goose while the Reader recites*)
READER
Praise to thee, Horus, son of Isis, son of Osiris, on this
                          auspicious day,
By the King of Upper and Lower Egypt, Heir-of-the-
Beneficent-Gods, Chosen-of-Ptah, Justiciar-of-Re,
Living-Image-of-Amun; the Son of Re, Ptolemaeus-
may-he-live-for-ever, Beloved-of-Ptah.
KING
He who has come in triumph, appearing in glory with his
                          Kindly Eye,
He has illumined the Two Lands with his beauty,
His Holy Eyes and his Darling Eyes being open.   60
He has burned up his enemies with his fiery breath,
He has swallowed their gore,
In order to restrain the body of him who is disloyal to him.
The flame, it consumes the body of him who plots against him.

CHORUS

Hurrah for Horus daily,   *65*
A joy to his father every day,
Who makes impotent him who turns the heart against him,
Who makes an end of him who trespasses against him.

READER

Triumphant over his enemies is Horus the Behdetite, great
god, lord of the sky.

CHORUS

Triumphant over his enemies is Horus the Behdetite, great
god, lord of the sky.   *70*

READER

Triumphant over his enemies is Horus the Behdetite, great
god, lord of the sky.

CHORUS

Triumphant over his enemies is Horus the Behdetite, great
god, lord of the sky.

READER

Triumphant over their enemies are Hathor, Mistress of
Denderah, and Thoth twice great, Lord of Hermopolis.

CHORUS

Triumphant over their enemies are Hathor, Mistress of
Denderah, and Thoth twice great, Lord of Hermopolis.

READER

Triumphant over their enemies are Hathor, Mistress of
Denderah, and Thoth twice great, Lord of Hermopolis.   *75*

CHORUS

Triumphant over their enemies are Hathor, Mistress of
Denderah, and Thoth twice great, Lord of Hermopolis.

READER

Triumphant over his enemies is the King of Upper and
Lower Egypt, Heir-of-the-Beneficent-Gods, Chosen-of-
Ptah, Justiciar-of-Re, Living-Image-of-Amun; the Son
of Re, Ptolemaeus-may-he-live-for-ever, Beloved-of-Ptah.

CHORUS

Triumphant over his enemies is the King of Upper and Lower
Egypt, Heir-of-the-Beneficent-Gods, Chosen-of-Ptah,
Justiciar-of-Re, Living-Image-of-Amun; the Son of Re,
Ptolemaeus-may-he-live-for-ever, Beloved-of-Ptah.

READER

Triumphant over his enemies is the King of Upper and Lower

Egypt, Heir-of-the-Beneficent-Gods, Chosen-of-Ptah,
Justiciar-of-Re, Living-Image-of-Amun; the Son of Re,
Ptolemaeus-may-he-live-for-ever, Beloved-of-Ptah.

CHORUS

Triumphant over his enemies is the King of Upper and
Lower Egypt, Heir-of-the-Beneficent-Gods, Chosen-of-
Ptah, Justiciar-of-Re, Living-Image-of-Amun; the Son of
Re, Ptolemaeus-may-he-live-for-ever, Beloved-of-Ptah.   *80*

READER

Horus in his strength has united the Two Lands;
Seth is overthrown in the form of a hippopotamus.
The Falcon-goddess is come to the House of Horus
And she says to her son Horus;

ISIS

Thy foes bow down and are destroyed for ever,   *85*
O thou Avenger of thy Father.
Come that I may instruct thee.
Consign his foreleg to the House of the Prince for thy
                    father Osiris, He-who-Awakes-Safely,
While his shank remains in Dep for thy great father Ipy-sehedj.
Let his shoulder be taken to Hermopolis for Thoth, the great
                                    one in the Valley.   *90*
Give his ribs to Great-of-Strength
And his breast to the Hare-goddess.
Give the great meat-portion of him to Khnum in the Temple,
His neck to Edjo of the Two Uraeus-goddesses, for she is
                                    thy great mother.
Give his thigh to Horus the Primordial One, the great god
                            who first came into being.   *95*
Give a roast of him to the birds which execute judgement in
                                    Djebawet.
Give his liver to Sepa
And his fat to the disease-demons of Dep.
Give his bones to the Khemu-iyet,
His heart to the Lower Egyptian Songstress.   *100*
Mine is his forepart, mine is his hinderpart, for I am thy
                            Mother whom he oppressed.
Give his tongue to the Young Harpooners,
The best of his inward parts to thy followers.
Take for thyself his heart and so assume the White Crown
                    and the kingly office of thy father Osiris.

What remains of him burn in the brazier of the Mistress of
the Two Lands.   *105*

CHORUS
Re has given to thee the strength of Mentu
And for thee, O Horus, is the jubilation.

Epilogue

READER
Horus the Behdetite, great god, lord of the sky, is
                              triumphant in the Broad Hall.
Overthrown are the enemies of his father Osiris.
  his mother Isis,
  his father Re,
  Thoth, master of hieroglyphic writing,
  the Ennead,
  the Great Palace,
  Abydos,
  Coptos,
  Hut-nuter,
  Wetjeset-Hor,
  Behdet,
  Denderah,
  Khant-Iabet
  And of His Majesty himself, the Son of
  Re, Ptolemaeus-may-he-live-for-ever,
  Beloved-of-Ptah.
CHORUS
  Overthrown are the enemies of His Majesty himself, the
  King of Upper and Lower Egypt, Lord of the Two Lands,
  Heir-of-the-Beneficent-Gods, Chosen-of-Ptah, Justiciar-
  of-Re, Living-Image-of-Amun; the Son of Re, Lord of
  Diadems, Ptolemaeus-may-he-live-for-ever, Beloved-of-
  Ptah, the Saviour-God.
  Overthrown are the enemies of His Majesty himself, the
  King of Upper and Lower Egypt, Lord of the Two
  Lands, Heir-of-the-Beneficent-Gods, Chosen-of-Ptah,
  Justiciar-of-Re, Living-Image-of-Amun; the Son of Re,
  Lord of Diadems, Ptolemaeus-may-he-live-for-ever,
  Beloved-of-Ptah, the Saviour-God.
  Overthrown are the enemies of His Majesty himself, the
  King of Upper and Lower Egypt, Lord of the Two

Lands, Heir-of-the-Beneficent-Gods, Chosen-of-Ptah,
Justiciar-of-Re, Living-Image-of-Amun; the Son of Re,
Lord of Diadems, Ptolemaeus-may-he-live-for-ever,
Beloved-of-Ptah, the Saviour God.

Overthrown are the enemies of His Majesty himself, the
King of Upper and Lower Egypt, Lord of the Two
Lands, Heir-of-the-Beneficent-Gods, Chosen-of-Ptah,
Justiciar-of-Re, Living-Image-of-Amun; the Son of Re,
Lord of Diadems, Ptolemaeus-may-he-live-for-ever,
Beloved-of-Ptah, the Saviour God.

FINIS

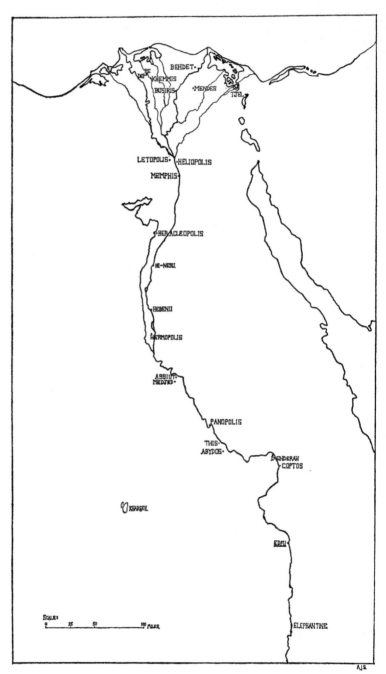

FIGURE 17 Sketch map of Egypt

Glossary

A. PLACES

ABYDOS   A very ancient city of Upper Egypt, for most of the historic period particularly closely associated with the worship of Osiris, who later was supposed to have been buried in the cenotaph of Djer (First Dynasty king).

ANDJET   A rare alternative name of Busiris (Djedu), the capital of the IXth (Busirite) Nome of Lower Egypt.

ASSIUT   Capital of the XIIIth nome (Lycopolite) of Upper Egypt. Its principal god was the jackal-god Wepwawet, 'the Opener of the Ways': an important guard and caravan post in Ancient Egypt.

BALCONY OF THE FALCON   One of the numerous names of the Temple of Edfu; also applied to the bridge linking the east and west wings of the Pylon where the Sacred Falcon was displayed annually after its election and coronation.

BEHDET   A sacred name of Edfu, capital of the IInd Nome of Upper Egypt; probably means 'Throne' or 'Seat'. Behdet does not seem to be the original name but was probably adopted because of the transfer of Horus the Behdetite to Edfu from his home town Behdet in the Delta: this may have happened as early as the Third Dynasty.

BROAD HALL   The hall in which the dead man was believed to be tried before Osiris and 42 assessors.

BUSIRIS   Capital of the IXth Lower Egyptian Nome, modern Abusir Bana in the central Delta. Traditionally regarded as the home of Osiris, who, however, drove out the original god Andjeti. Busiris is the Greek form of *Per-Usir* 'House of Osiris' but the regular name of the city was Djedu.

BUTO   Modern Tell el Farain north west Delta, VIth nome of Lower Egypt. An important religious and political centre, composed of the twin towns of Pe and Dep, capital of the predynastic kingdom of the Delta. Principal deity was the uraeus-goddess Edjo.

COASTS OF HORUS   A name of Egypt.

COPTOS   Capital of the Vth Upper Egyptian Nome; modern Qift: principal god was the fertility god Min.

DENDERAH   Capital of the VIth Upper Egyptian Nome. Principal centre of the cult of Hathor.

DEP   One of the twin cities Pe and Dep that composed the ancient Delta city Buto. Dep was the town particularly associated with the goddess Edjo (Uto).

DJEBA   The ancient official secular name of Edfu and origin, through Coptic Etbo, of the modern Arabic Edfu. The literal meaning of the name is

'Retribution-Town', hence the punning allusion to 'retribution, punishment' in reference to this name.

DJEBAWET   A town with a cult of Horus, presumably at or near Buto. The mention of 'the birds which execute judgement' (III.iii.96) is probably a reference to the heron cult at Djebawet.

ELEPHANTINE   The southernmost town of Egypt proper on the island of the same name opposite modern Assuan; capital of the Ist Upper Egyptian nome. At its south end was an ancient fortress, an outpost against Nubia and the South. The principal god was Khnum, associated with the goddesses Anukis and Satis.

FORTRESS, The   A not uncommon name of Egypt in the inscriptions of Edfu. The concept of Egypt as the inviolable, impregnable fortress is one of the reactions to foreign domination.

GREAT PALACE   The temple of the sun-god at Heliopolis.

GREAT SEAT   One of the names of Edfu and also of the Sanctuary of the temple. In our play (II.ii.10) there is little doubt that the allusion is to Edfu.

HEBENU   Capital of the XVIth (Oryx) Nome of Upper Egypt, probably to be identified with Kom el Ahmar or Zawiyet el Maitin (Zawiyet el Amwat) a few miles south of Minia in Middle Egypt, on the right bank. Associated with Horus: in the Late Period the nome-sign is often written with a falcon (Horus) on the back of an oryx, which itself was a Sethian animal. In the Legend of the Winged Disk it was the site of a big victory of Horus the Behdetite over Seth and his followers.

HELIOPOLIS   Capital of the XIIIth Nome of Lower Egypt, principal centre of the sun-cult and Re in Egypt. The ancient site, at Matarieh a few miles north east of Cairo, is devastated and little remains apart from the obelisk of Sesostris I. Egyptian name was Iunu, the On of the Bible.

HE-NESU   Identified with Kom el Ahmar Sawaris, on the right bank of the Nile 5 km south of Sharunah. While its identification is reasonably assured, the ancient texts are contradictory: in the XIIth Dynasty it is said to be metropolis of the XVIIIth Falcon Nome (Upper Egypt); the great Edfu Nome List records it as metropolis of the XVIIth (Dog) Nome.

HERACLEOPOLIS   Capital of XXth Upper Egyptian Nome, near entrance to Fayum, modern Ehnasieh el Medinah. Chief god was the ram-headed Herishef, Arsaphes.

HERMOPOLIS   Metropolis of the XVth (Hare) Nome, Upper Egypt: ancient Khemenu 'City of the Eight', modern El Ashmunein. Principal centre of the cult of Thoth.

HOUSE OF THE PRINCE (or perhaps House of the Great One).   Probably a part of the temple of Re at Heliopolis.

HUT-NETER   Name of the 'holy mound' of Neref, the necropolis of Heracleopolis.

IYET   Name of the place where the sacred trees of the IInd Lower Egyptian nome (Letopolite) were worshipped.

KENSET   A name of Nubia not uncommon in texts of the Graeco-Roman
Period.

KHANT-IABET   'Front of the East', capital of the XIVth (Tanite) nome of
Lower Egypt. Its capital was Tjel, Sile, the great north-eastern frontier
fortress of Egypt, modern Tell Abu Sefah, 3 km east of Kantara on the
Suez Canal. Its local god, identified with Horus the Behdetite, was a lion
whose special function was to protect Egypt against Asiatics and
foreigners.

KHARGEH   Egyptian name Kenmet, is the southernmost of the six great
oases to the west of Egypt proper.

KHEMMIS   A mythical island in the Delta marshes near Buto in which Isis
was supposed to have given birth to and reared Horus.

KHENT-HEN-NUFER   An ancient name of Nubia. Note that in 1.iii.21 Horus
is called 'Nubian in Khent-hen-nufer.' This is because at one time Edfu
was the southern frontier town of Egypt and there may have been a time
when the inhabitants of Edfu and its nome were regarded as little more
than Nubians, cf. the strong Nubian element, exclusive of the people
displaced by the flooding of Nubia, in southern Upper Egypt. It is
exceptional for Horus to be called 'Nubian' but it is less surprising that
Seth also (III.ii.3) is called 'the Nubian.'

LETOPOLIS   Egyptian Khem, modern Ausim, 13 km north west of Cairo, was
capital of the IInd Lower Egyptian nome. Its god was a warlike form of
Horus, worshipped as a falcon idol. The heads of the enemies of Horus
were said to be cut off here.

MANSION OF THE FALCON   One of the names of the Temple of Edfu.

MEDJED   A cult centre of Hathor and Tefnut: identified with modern
Dronkah, 5 km south west of Assiut.

MEMPHIS   Capital of the Ist Lower Egyptian nome, a very important
political and religious centre. Principal centre of the cult of Ptah, said to
have been founded by Menes, the founder of the First Dynasty and capital
of Egypt in the earliest dynasties. Memphis is derived from Men-nefer, a
name which is not used in the play which uses either 'White Wall'
(ineb-hedj) a very old name (1.iii.46) or the rare Kha-nefer (1.iii.58).
Both forms have been translated in this book as Memphis.

MENDES   Egyptian Djedet (to be distinguished from Djedu, one of the
names of Busiris), modern Tell er-Ruba, almost in the centre of the Delta.
Centre of the cult to a ram-god, fertility god.

MESEN   One of the names of Edfu, and also of a chapel in the temple
immediately behind the Sanctuary. There was also a Mesen in the Delta
(cf. Prologue 28.29): identification is complicated and uncertain, for
while remains of a Ramesside temple of Horus Lord of Mesen have been
found at Tjel (see above under Khant-Iabet) the texts also mention an
eastern and western Mesen in the Delta. In the play Mesen should be
assumed to refer always to Edfu, unless the Delta connection is explicitly
mentioned.

NOME 'province, district.'

NOME-OF-HIM-WITH-THE-OUTSPREAD-TALONS XVIIIth nome of Upper Egypt; its capital was at one time He-nesu.

ORYX NOME XVIth Upper Egyptian nome, whose capital was Hebenu.

PANOPOLIS Modern Akhmim, chief town of the IXth Upper Egyptian nome. Principal divinities Min-Horus and Isis.

PATHS OF HORUS Either the great military road from Egypt into Western Asia or a fortress on that road (probably Tjel, Sile, *cf*. Khant-Iabet).

PE One of the two towns that formed the city of Buto (Tell el Farain in the north west Delta). Pe was the residence of Horus, whereas the twin city Dep was particularly associated with the goddess Edjo.

POOL OF HORUS The Sacred Lake of the Temple of Edfu on which the action of the play was supposed to take place.

RETRIBUTION-TOWN See Djeba.

RIVER BANKS A frequent epithet or name of Egypt.

THIS Capital of the VIIIth nome of Upper Egypt, probably to be identified with modern Girga or a place in its neighbourhood; according to Manetho it was the home town of Menes and the kings of the first two dynasties. Its god was Onuris, whose consort was the lion-headed goddess Mehit.

TWO LANDS A very common designation of Egypt, which was composed of two lands—Upper and Lower Egypt.

TWO OUTPOURINGS A name of Egypt. According to one Egyptian view there were two Niles, an Upper and a Lower Egyptian, whose sources were at Elephantine (or in its neighbourhood) and Heliopolis. Thus the Outpouring of Seth (Kebeh Seth) was Upper Egypt and the Outpouring of Horus (Kebeh Hor) was Lower Egypt.

WETJESET-HOR (also WETJESET) A common name of Edfu.

YEBT An infrequent name of Hermopolis Magna.

B. PERSONS (HUMAN AND DIVINE) AND THINGS

AMUN The principal god of Thebes; in the Middle and New Kingdom the most powerful of all gods; also associated with Re, hence the names Amen-Re and Amen-Re King of the Gods. He was essentially a creator and fertility god, god of the air and breath of life.

BARK OF THE MORNING The great boat in which the sun-god was supposed to sail across the sky by day.

BE A common name of Seth in Graeco-Roman hieroglyphic texts.

CAITIFF An insulting name applied to Seth.

CLEOPATRA In the version of the play at Edfu she was the wife of Ptolemy VIII, Euergetes II, and mother of Ptolemy IX, Soter II: see above p. 16.

CROWN The two crowns particularly mentioned in the play are the Red

Crown of Lower Egypt and the tall, conical White Crown of Upper Egypt. These two crowns were combined to form the Double Diadem: see below.

DESES-FISH   An unidentified fish.

DISEASE-DEMONS-OF DEP   Among the causes of disease recognised by the Egyptians were evil spirits or demons. Particularly common were the messengers of the goddess Sekhmet who were supposed to bring pestilence, death and famine (*cf.* II.ii.57). The Disease-demons of Dep are not attested in other texts.

DOUBLE DIADEM   The White Crown and the Red Crown when combined formed the Double Diademm—Egyptian Pa-Sekhemty (Pschent) 'The Two Powerful Ones'—worn by the King in his capacity of King of Upper and Lower Egypt. It was regularly worn by Horus the Behdetite.

EDJO   The uraeus-goddess of Buto. Since Buto was the capital of the predynastic kingdom of the Delta, Edjo and the uraeus throughout Egyptian history represented Lower Egypt in contrast with Nekhbet, the vulture-goddess of Hierakonpolis, who represented Upper Egypt. The uraeus was supposed to spit fire against the enemies of the King.

ENNEAD   The nine gods (the Great Ennead) of the theological system of Heliopolis. At their head was Atum who produced from himself Shu (air, atmosphere) and Tefnut (moisture), who begat Geb (earth) and Nut (sky). The union of Geb and Nut resulted in the birth of Osiris, Isis, Seth and Nephthys. There was also a Small Ennead of lesser divinities which never played an important part in Egyptian religion.

FEN-GODDESS   Appears often in the processions of the so-called Nile-gods in Graeco-Roman temples. The marshes that border the agricultural land are her domain and hence she is the mistress of game, particularly of fish and fowl.

FEN-MEN, The Young Fen-Men   A general designation of the harpooners and young men who supported Horus in his struggle with Seth.

FIFTEENTH-DAY FEAST   Full moon festival, fifteenth day of the lunar month.

GEB   The earth-god, often depicted as a prostrate figure on whose back all creation lives and grows. His wife was Nut, the sky-goddess, and their children were Osiris, Isis, Seth and Nephthys.

GODDESS OF RAIMENT   Egyptian Djayet: a goddess connected with cloth and clothing.

GODDESS OF WEAVING   The goddess Tayet, goddess of spinning and weaving, who therefore provided bandages, ceremonial garments and materials used in ritual. Her consort was Hedjhotpe. Sometimes Re is said to be her father, through her identification with Great-of-Magic, but elsewhere she is identified with Isis, hence Nut is said to be her mother; the King sometimes said to be her son.

HARAKHTE   A name of the sun-god in Heliopolis, hence the form Re-Harakhte. Originally the name appears to have meant 'Horus of the

Horizon' but from at least the Eighteenth Dynasty the name was usually interpreted as 'Horus of the Two Horizons'.

HAR-KHENTEKHTAI Usually depicted as a falcon-god, hence as a form of Horus, with chief cult centre at Athribis in the Delta. In the play he is referred to as helmsman of the gods (I.v. 32 and *cf* p. 42 above).

HARE-GODDESS Egyptian Unwet: goddess of Unu 'Hare-town' original capital of the XVth (Hare) Nome of Upper Egypt, later identified in whole or part with Hermopolis.

HAROERIS 'Horus the Elder': a falcon-god whose principal cult centres were Letopolis, Kus and Kom Ombo. In spite of his name, he was not an ancient god and was probably created as a counterbalance to Har-pa-khered (Harpocrates) 'Horus the Child'.

HARPOONERS (also the YOUNG HARPOONERS): a general term for the followers and supporters of Horus in his fights with Seth.

HATHOR The principal goddess of Denderah, though she was worshipped in many other places. She was the wife of Horus the Behdetite, their marriage being one of the great annual festivals of Edfu. Her nature is very complex: goddess of song, music, love and dance, she also had a special cow form and at Thebes in particular was important in funerary religion. In the Late Period she and Isis were often virtually one person.

HEDJHOTPE God of weaving and clothing; consort of Tayet, goddess of spinning and weaving.

HE-WHO-WAKES-SAFELY A name of Osiris.

HIM-WITH-THE-UPRAISED-ARM In Egyptian religious texts this is the characteristic epithet of Min; in the play it obviously refers to Horus the Behdetite, probably with no other significance than a reference to the raising of the arm of Horus as he harpooned the hippopotamus.

HIM-WHO-IS-ON-THE-MOUND Possibly an epithet of Horus: *cf* the words of Isis to Horus 'See thou art on a mound free of bushes' (I.ii.19).

HORUS THE BEHDETITE The falcon-god of Edfu, usually depicted as a man with falcon's head wearing the Double Diadem. Though originally a god of the Delta, he became the epitome of Upper Egypt with chief cult centre at Edfu (Behdet). In the Late Period he combines the roles of a solar god, the god of Upper Egypt, the royal god par excellence, and the enemy of Seth. Though originally distinct from Horus, the son of Isis and Osiris, inevitably the two gods were confused the one with the other.

HORUS THE PRIMORDIAL ONE A somewhat infrequent designation of Horus the Behdetite, who nevertheless is called at Edfu 'Eldest Son of the Eight Primeval Gods', 'Heir of the Eight Primeval Gods' and 'Over-lord of the First Primordial Gods'.

IMHOTEP Chief minister and architect of King Zoser of the Third Dynasty. Subsequently he acquired the reputation of a wise man and in the Late Period was deified, as Imhotep the Great, Son of Ptah, and worshipped as a God of medecine, identified with Asklepios. According to Edfu tradition he was author of the 'Book of Designing a Temple' on which the plan of Edfu Temple was based. In Act III, Scene iii (and possibly throughout the play) the Reader impersonated him.

IPY-SEHEDJ   An unknown divinity.

ISIS   One of the four children of Geb and Nut; sister and wife of Osiris, mother of Horus.

KHEMU-IYET, literally 'Those who know not coming', otherwise unknown divine beings.

KHENTEKHTAI: see Har-Khentekhtai.

KHNUM   Ram-headed creator and fertility god. Principal god of Elephantine and the Cataract region, and of Esna; fashioned mankind on the potter's wheel.

KING   In theory the King in *The Triumph of Horus* was the reigning king of Egypt; in fact in the surviving text the King was Ptolemy IX, Soter II.

LADY OF THE CHASE   Patroness of the chase, more particularly of the catching, of fish and fowl.

LORD OF MESEN   Since Mesen was a name of Edfu and of a city in the Delta, possibly Tjel (see above p. 125, Mesen), the identity of the Lord of Mesen is not always easy to establish. In the Prologue 9, he is undoubtedly Horus the Behdetite. But throughout the play Horus Lord of Mesen is the representative of Lower Egypt in contrast with Horus the Behdetite, representative of Upper Egypt.

LOWER EGYPTIAN BULL   A designation of the hippopotamus, identified with Seth. Though in early times Seth is especially linked with Upper Egypt, his cult appears to have been well-established in certain places in the north-eastern Delta. Hippopotami seem to have been more common in the swamps and marshes of the Delta than in Upper Egypt.

LOWER EGYPTIAN SONGSTRESS   Together with the Upper Egyptian Songstress she was the goddess responsible for music and song in temple cult and ritual.

MARAUDER   Seth as hippopotamus.

MASTER OF THE BIRD-POOL   A title of Khnum.

MASTER OF THE UNIVERSE   A title of Atum of Heliopolis.

MENTU   Falcon-headed god of Hermonthis, modern Armant: prior to the rise of Amun was principal god of the Theban nome; a war-god.

MIN   Fertility god and also lord of the eastern deserts; principal cult centres were Coptos and Akhmim.

NEHES, variant PNEHES   A name of Seth.

NEPHTHYS   One of the four children of Geb and Nut (see above under Ennead) and sister and wife of Seth. Nevertheless, her link with Seth was slight: she supported Osiris and Isis against Seth, and Osiris is even said to have been father of her son Anubis.

NUBIAN   A term applied in the play to both Horus the Behdetite (I.iii.21) and Seth (III.ii.3): *cf* above p. 125, Khent-hen-nufer.

NURSE   A cow or cow-goddess who acted as nurse of divine children.

NUT   Goddess of the sky, wife of Geb (earth) and mother of Osiris, Isis, Seth and Nephthys.

ONNOPHRIS   Greek form of Egyptian Wenen-nefer 'The Good Being': a
common epithet of Osiris.

ONURIS   God of This, a hunter and warrior. His name means 'He who
brings back the Distant One' and refers to his role in the legend of
bringing back the Moon, the Eye of Horus which had been taken from him.

OSIRIS   The great Egyptian god of the dead. One of the four children of
Geb and Nut, husband of his sister Isis and father of Horus.

PERVERSE ONE   An insulting designation of Seth.

PNEHES   See Nehes.

PROTOTYPE MAN   An approximate translation of a name applied to Horus in
the texts of Edfu and which, literally translated, may perhaps mean
'Man of the First Lotus Leaf' (an alternative rendering 'Man of the First
Thousand' is now, I think, unlikely). Unpublished evidence shows
that a group of 28 gods or demi-gods, who were active in the creation of
the world and the temple, bore this name.

PTAH   The principal god of Memphis; artisan of the gods, patron of artisans,
fashioner of all things.

PTOLEMAEUS (Ptolemy)   Ptolemy IX, Soter II, son of Ptolemy VIII, Euergetes
II and Cleopatra III: see above pp. 16–17. He is the 'King' in the surviving
Edfu version of the play.

QUEEN   In the Edfu version of the play she is Cleopatra III, wife of Ptolemy
VIII and mother of Ptolemy IX and X: see above p. 16.

RE   The sun-god of Heliopolis.

SABET-Snakes   The name probably means 'multi-coloured snakes' and
probably refers to cobras; their mistress was the goddess Hathor. The
Interlude in Act I, Scene iv refers to an ancient legend according to which
the enemies of Horus were beheaded in Letopolis; as early as the Pyramid
Texts these enemies were called *sabet*-snakes.

SCORPION OF BEHDET   An epithet of Isis.

SEKHMET   'The Powerful One', a goddess with the head of a lioness, wife
of Ptah at Memphis. A warlike, dread goddess who personifies the
destructive powers of nature and who, with the assistance of her
messengers (*cf* p. 127 above, Disease Demons of Dep), brought pestilence
and death to the enemies of the King.

SEPA   An ancient god of Heliopolis, represented as a centipede. From early
times he was regarded as a protector against harmful and evil beings and
animals; in later times he was assimilated to Osiris.

SETH   Originally overlord of Upper Egypt and brother of Horus with whom
he fought for rule over all Egypt. Later considered as brother of Osiris,
and hence uncle of Horus; he murdered Osiris the good king; ultimately
Horus avenged his father and regained his birthright (see above pp. 28–29).
Throughout the greater part of Egyptian history, but to varying degrees,
he was the god of the desert and of foreign lands and the personification
of evil.

SHESMU   A god who had two rather different principal aspects: on the one hand he was god of the oil- and wine-press; on the other he was an avenging and bloodthirsty god who bound sinners and enemies of the gods to the execution block. He was also a star-god.

SOKAR   The god of the Memphite necropolis, hence its modern name Saqqarah; usually depicted as a mummified falcon or a mummiform human with falcon's head; naturally came to be very closely linked with Osiris. His close association with Ptah led to his being regarded as a patron of workmen and to his reputation as a worker in metals, hence the claim that he forged the weapons of Horus (II.ii.73).

SOPD   A warlike god, guardian of the eastern marches of the Delta; often depicted as a falcon-idol, hence his close association with Horus. He is also depicted as a Beduin and hence is lord of the routes across the north-eastern desert and the lands to which they lead.

SOTHIS   The dog-star Sirius, whose heliacal rising was considered by the Egyptians to mark the beginning of the annual inundation and of the Egyptian year; was very early identified with Isis.

TAYET   Goddess of spinning and weaving; maker and provider of various ceremonial garments and bandages. Edfu texts identify her sometimes with Great-of-Magic with Re as father, and sometimes with Isis and hence as daughter of Nut. Her consort was Hedjhotpe, god of weaving and clothing (see above p. 127, Goddess of Weaving).

TEFNUT   In the creation myth of Heliopolis was considered as 'moisture', daughter of Atum, hence sister and wife of Shu (air, atmosphere): see above p. 127, under Ennead. Is sometimes represented as a lioness.

TERRIBLE FACE   A not uncommon designation of Seth in the guise of a crocodile.

THOSE-WHO-ARE-IN-THE-WATER   A general term to describe all those who assisted Seth in his wars against Horus. In the Edfu texts they are usually crocodiles; sometimes are hippopotami; sometimes both crocodiles and hippopotami. In II.i.27.80 they are certainly crocodiles; in I.i.42, since there is no determinative, their precise nature is uncertain.

THOTH   God of wisdom and writing, said to be inventor of writing and master of hieroglyphic writing; moon-god. Though possibly of Delta origin, his principal cult-centre came to be Hermopolis Magna (Ashmunein); his sacred animals were the ibis and the baboon.

UNSUCCESSFUL ONE   A contemptuous epithet of Seth.

URAEUS   A cobra, identified with the goddess Edjo of Buto. Since Buto was the capital of the predynastic kingdom of the Delta, the uraeus represented Lower Egypt and as such was worn in the royal crown together with the head of the vulture as representative of Upper Egypt (Nekhbet was the vulture goddess of Hierakonpolis, prehistoric capital of Upper Egypt). The uraeus was supposed to spit fire against the enemies of the King.

WEARY-HEARTED ONE   A designation of Osiris.

WENTY   A form of Horus as conqueror of Seth. He is depicted most frequently as Horus on a bull, sometimes as a man on a bull, or as Horus on a crocodile, or as a falcon on an oryx. All these variant writings exemplify the fact that Horus has the supremacy over Seth.

WEPWAWET 'the Opener of the Ways', the jackal-god of Assiut.

Appendix A

Second Thoughts on the Edfu Stage

The manuscript of this book had been completed when, for the first time, I met Mr Arnold Hare at the National Drama Conference to whom I had been giving an account of *The Triumph of Horus*. To Mr Hare's query whether I thought there was any connection between my suggested stage-setting of the Edfu play and the mediaeval theatre in the round I had to confess that I knew nothing about the latter. Mr Hare suggested that I might profitably consult Richard Southern, *The Mediaeval Theatre in the Round* (Faber, 1957). This, after a slight delay, I was able to do and it led me to delve more deeply into the subject of the early stage.

The first impression of a hasty glance through Dr Southern's fascinating study was that any resemblances that one might suggest may have existed between Edfu and the theatre in the round were superficial and unimportant. The differences in the setting, in the times of the performances and in the actors seemed so fundamental that it was difficult to imagine that there was any true similarity. The 'Scaffolds' in particular appeared to present insuperable difficulties. And then, suddenly, it was realised that there were details in the Edfu reliefs which, though perfectly familiar, had not received proper consideration. The results of these second thoughts are so interesting and so totally unexpected that it was felt that they merited separate treatment, all the more so since they may perhaps throw new light on the presentation of the Edfu play.

The mediaeval theatre in the round consisted essentially of a circular area of greensward. The Cornish plays, for instance, appear to have been performed within circular earthworks, probably prehistoric fortifications, near the towns. If no such natural amphitheatre existed, it seems probable that a ditch was dug round a circular area, the earth from the ditch being thrown up on the inside of the circle, or, if a ditch was not feasible, the area may have been delimited by a stout timber palisade. The area thus enclosed was called the 'Place' and on it much of the action of the play took place. The surrounding earth was called the 'Hill'. The surviving plans of some of these mediaeval plays suggest that at various points round the circle, probably on the Hill itself, were erected a number of 'Scaffolds' supporting booths or mansions, apparently draped at back, sides and top but sometimes, at least, having in front a draw-curtain. These Scaffolds served the purpose of stages for one or more actors, who could also sometimes descend to, or ascend from, the Place by means of a wooden ladder. Some Scaffolds also accommodated privileged spectators or even an orchestra. The audience may have sat on the Hill (Dr Southern aptly quotes the analogy of The Hill at Sydney Cricket Ground) but evidently many members of the audience were allowed to occupy restricted areas around the Scaffolds and appear to have moved from Scaffold to Scaffold as the action of the play developed. The action of the play took place on the Scaffolds or in the Place itself in which, if need arose as in *The Castle of Perseverance*, could be erected such properties as a house or a castle.

If we now turn to the Edfu reliefs, it will be noted that in the Prologue (fig. 6) and in all the scenes of Acts I and II (figs. 7–13), but not in Act III (figs. 14–16), there is always to one side or other of the Sacred Lake at least one rectangular block, always higher than the rim of the lake, on which stands one or more of the actors. Most frequently it is the King who is shown standing on a block or pedestal, which is always to the left of the lake: sometimes his arms hang by his side (figs. 7, 9, 11) or are raised in adoration (figs. 8, 10); sometimes he is harpooning the hippopotamus (figs. 6, 12). Once (fig. 12) the stand is big enough to accommodate the King and the Young Harpooners. In another scene (fig. 13) the Queen is shown on a block to the left of the lake while Horus the Behdetite stands on another pedestal to the right of the lake.

Other rectangular blocks or pedestals are to be seen in some of the reliefs of the Legend of the Winged Disk which, as we have seen (p. 15 and fig. 1) occupy the second register immediately above the scenes of *The Triumph of Horus*: we will return to these scenes a little later (p. 139 below). The use of these blocks in these two groups of texts is so unusual that it must surely be deliberate and significant. Though the Graeco-Roman temples of Egypt are not yet completely published, line-drawings and photographs of several thousand ritual and festival scenes have been printed. A somewhat hasty survey of these shows that the reliefs of the Myth of Horus at Edfu are exceptional. The general rule appears to be that if the divinities who receive the offering are standing, their feet are always on the same base line as the King, who acts as officiant. If a god is seated, he is always on a throne placed on a low pedestal and the King stands before him on the base line: the pedestal, it is clear, only acts as a support for the god's throne. Standing gods appear to be characteristic of the first register; gods seated on thrones are characteristic of the second and other registers. My search through the drawings has been extensive, though it does not claim to be exhaustive. At Edfu the only exceptions so far observed occur in the astronomical texts and the texts of the hours of the day in the frieze of the outer hypostyle in which the reliefs depict the King, often harpooning one of the enemies of the bark, or a god, or a group of minor divinities standing on pedestals.[1] At Denderah I have only noted one example in the halls of the main temple,[2] but there are a few more instances in the Crypts[3] and the Roman Mammisi.[4] In all these scenes at Denderah the King always kneels on the same block that supports the throne of the god and presents an offering: there is no parallel with the Edfu scenes that interest us.

If it be suggested that the pedestal is merely a device to show honour to a god or a king, the answer is that such a device is not employed in the regular ritual scenes in the temples. Particularly instructive in this connection is the first of the scenes of the Legend of the Winged Disk (fig. 18: for the position of the scene see fig. 1, Register II, Relief 5). Here the King is performing the rite of 'Uplifting the Sky': he raises on high the sky over which is the winged scarab representing Horus the Behdetite: the King and the naos containing Horus the Behdetite and Re-Harakhte seated on a throne are on pedestals. If, however, we look at other examples of this rite,[5] no pedestal is used, the King and divinities always stand on the base line. Honorific reasons, therefore, are no explanation.

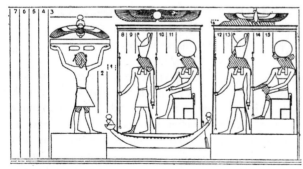

FIGURE 18   Edfu, West Enclosure Wall: Register II, Relief 5

The conclusion appears inevitable that the use of these **blocks** or pedestals was deliberate and must be connected with the play. No hint is given as to the construction of the pedestals: they are invariably depicted as solid and one is entitled to assume that they were made either of stone or of brick plastered and whitewashed to imitate stone. All the pedestals are of the same height and are approximately one third of the height of a man: if the artist was working to scale (and, of course, there is no guarantee of this), it might be suggested that perhaps each pedestal was not more than 18–24 inches in height.

If these conclusions be accepted, it is possible to amplify somewhat the tentative hints as to stage and setting that have been given above in Chapter 2. It will be noted that the reliefs invariably place the gods on the right of the Sacred Lake, from the point of view of the onlooker, and King and Queen on the left. The pedestals of the King and Horus must have been very close to the edge of the lake to enable them, when need arose, to mime the harpooning of the hippopotamus (unless we have to assume, contrary to the evidence of the reliefs, that at each harpooning the King and Horus descended from their pedestals). The pedestal of the King must presumably have been larger than the others since in Act II, Scene i (fig. 12) it apparently accommodated the Young Harpooners also. It seems not impossible that such characters as Isis and Thoth in all probability may have stood on their own individual pedestals to the right of the lake, but this is guess work since their pedestals are never depicted. Similarly, it is possible to suggest that the Reader may also have stood on a pedestal, probably to the left of the Queen, possibly slightly advanced in order the more easily to control the Chorus and the general development of the action: once again, this is a guess and cannot be proved. It also seems essential to assume that there should have been a pedestal for Horus Lord of Mesen between Horus the Behdetite and Isis. It is thus possible to suggest a basic lay-out for the main characters in the Prologue and Acts I and II:

| Reader | Queen | King | Sacred Lake | Horus the Behdetite | Horus Lord of Mesen | Isis | Thoth |

No booth or naos is ever depicted on any pedestal and there is no hint of any kind of screening. We thus have to imagine that the principal actors stood in full view on their pedestals. There is no hint as to the position of such minor characters as the Demons: possibly they entered only for those scenes in which they had a part to play. Similarly, precise evidence as to the position of the Chorus is completely lacking but it had such an important part to play that it must have been on stage all the time, probably in the area in front of the Sacred Lake and the pedestals of the principal actors but not on a pedestal of its own.

Recognition of the fact that *The Triumph of Horus* employed a number of pedestals, elementary multiple stages, raises the question of movement in the play. One has the impression that, compared with a modern play, movement must have been relatively restricted; some of the actors may well have had to stand on their pedestals throughout the play. Nevertheless, it is evident that at times some of the actors must have descended from their pedestals and boarded the boat, as for example Horus the Behdetite and Isis in the Prologue (see p. 43 above), and Horus the Behdetite and Thoth in Act II, Scene ii (see p. 31 above). It is also reasonable to suggest that the Demons in the scenes of Act I, the Young Harpooners in Act II, Scene i, the Upper and Lower Egyptian Princesses in Act II, Scene ii, and the gods and goddesses in the dismemberment scenes in Act III only appeared for those scenes, or parts of scenes, in which they had a part to play. If all these actors had been on stage all the time, the 'stage' surely would have been very congested and crowded and there would have been a real danger of impairing the important visual aspect of the whole play.

The use of pedestals, however, suggests that there must have been more movement than one might have, at first, been inclined to suggest. Consideration of how Act I ought to be presented will illustrate this point. Here we know that the Sacred Lake occupied the centre of the stage and one is bound to assume that at the beginning of each scene the principals were to be seen to left and right of the lake on their pedestals. It would have been pointless for Horus the Behdetite and Horus Lord of Mesen to have performed their harpoonings by stabbing at empty air while the boat and the lake, in which the hippopotamus was supposed to be, remained idle and empty. One is forced, therefore, to suggest that in each scene first Horus Lord of Mesen descended from his pedestal and, accompanied by the appropriate Demon, boarded the boat and then, having performed the first harpooning, returned to his pedestal while Horus the Behdetite and the second Demon boarded the boat and mimed the second harpooning, and so on.

Mr Poole, in fact, has suggested to me that the text of the play itself may at two points contain hints of even more movement. The first of these occurs in Act I, Scene ii, when Isis says:

> Cast thy harpoon, I pray thee,
> At the mound of the Savage Beast.
> See, thou art on a mound clear of bushes,
> A shore free from scrub. (I.ii.17–20)

Here I confess to being uncertain. Mr Poole's suggestion is not impossible but I am bound to point out that these words may also be interpreted merely as a form of verbal scene-setting: this is a typical and ancient device employed, for example, superbly and rather differently in the Prologue to Shakespeare's *King Henry V*.

Mr Poole's second example is to be found in the opening words of the Chorus in Act II, Scene i:

> Come, let us hasten to the Pool of Horus,
> That we may see the Falcon in his ship,
> That we may see the Son of Isis in his war-galley,
> Like Re in the Bark of the Morning. (II.i.1–4)

Here again there is an element of scene-setting but I admit that I am with Mr Poole and am prepared to recognise here an indication of movement on the part of the Chorus. In fact, in the Padgate production Mr Poole at this point moved the Chorus from their lower stage positions to the upper stage. A closer study of the text of the play from the multiple stage angle might well reveal other instances.

In Act III it will be noticed (figs. 14–16) no pedestals are depicted. The action of this Act, involving as it does a mime and two dismemberments of the hippopotamus, was quite different from that of the two previous Acts. All must have been performed on the ground, presumably in front of the Sacred Lake so that the audience should have an unimpeded view of what was taking place. The chief actors, it may perhaps be suggested, possibly returned to their pedestals when the more physical actions had been concluded: thus in Act III, Scene iii the King may have descended from his pedestal only for the pouring of the grain into the mouth of the goose.

Here it may be pointed out that since, as we have remarked above (pp. 52, 56), much of the spoken words of the play must have been heard incompletely, if at all, by most of the audience, and since even if the words could have been heard, they must have been to a large extent incomprehensible because of the language employed, the play must have depended heavily on its visual impact for its effect. Granted that the audience was enthusiastic and deeply involved, granted that the audience knew the theme, the story and the meaning, it is difficult for us to imagine such a play holding the audience unless the visual aspect was carefully planned and stressed. It is this that may have motivated the employment of the pedestals and in such circumstances movement would certainly have been an important reinforcement of the visual element. One may quote here a modern writer's words about the pageant theatres of the streets in the Middle Ages: ' . . . the primary appeal of these occasional festivals, then as now, was visual. If the "very

important persons" who occupied the best positions in this rudi-
mentary "auditorium" could be regarded as grounded in Latin and
English, the majority of the spectators could not. Elaborate precautions
were therefore taken to ensure that the significance of the occasion
was visible to all: for, as Volumnia observes to Coriolanus in a more
urgent context, "the eyes of the ignorant" are "more learned than
the ears".[6]

We have already mentioned above (p. 134) that pedestals are also to
be observed in some of the scenes of the Legend of the Winged Disk
(see p. 15). It is essential, therefore, to give some account of these
scenes, for whose position and order see fig. 1, Register II, Reliefs 5–12.
One or more pedestals are depicted in six of these eight reliefs, i.e. in
Reliefs 5, 6, 8, 9, 11, 12. There appears to be some element of design
here, for each pair of scenes with pedestals is separated by one without:
it is as yet unknown whether this arrangement had any special significance. In each scene a Main Text in vertical columns is to be found to
the left of the relief and in all but Relief 5 (fig. 18) three horizontal
lines over the relief itself record the first part of the Main Text. The
arrangement of the pedestals is so complicated that a relatively simple
description, as in *The Triumph of Horus*, is not possible and we give a
summary description of each.

Relief 5 (fig. 18). On the right is a pedestal on which is a naos in which
Horus the Behdetite stands in front of a seated Re-Harakhte: both gods
face to the left. In front of the naos is a sacred bark in which is another
naos with standing Horus the Behdetite and seated Re-Harakhte, both
facing to the left. Finally, at the extreme left, the King on a pedestal
faces the gods and holds aloft the sky.

FIGURE 19   Edfu, West Enclosure Wall: Register II, Relief 8

Relief 6. On the right is the goddess Astarte in a chariot; in the centre is a bark and in it stand, from left to right, Horus the Behdetite and Isis before Re-Harakhte seated on a throne: all three gods face to the left. At the extreme left, standing on a pedestal facing the gods, is a human figure called 'The Goodly Harpooner who stands in front'. Both the Harpooner and Horus the Behdetite harpoon an object now destroyed, probably a crocodile.

Relief 8 (fig. 19). On the right is a boat in which stands Re-Harakhte; in front of him Horus the Behdetite with his right hand harpoons a crocodile(?) while holding in his left hand two ropes, one attached to the harpoon and the other to a human figure who is being harpooned by Horus son of Isis, standing on a pedestal. Standing on the same pedestal as Horus son of Isis are Isis herself and behind her Thoth, who holds four human beings in fetters.

Relief 9. On the right is a boat in which is a naos with a seated figure of Re-Harakhte, facing to the left. In front of the boat is a large pedestal on which are, from right to left, Horus the Behdetite and Horus son of Isis who harpoon a human figure kneeling between them; Isis; and a naos in which is a mummiform figure of Osiris.

Relief 11. On the left is a boat in full sail in which stands 'The Harpooner of Horus, prow-man in his war-galley'. The Harpooner holds with his right hand a harpoon with which he transfixes a crocodile and in his left holds a rope attached to the prow of a second boat. In the prow of the latter stands Horus the Behdetite as he harpoons a crocodile; behind Horus stands Thoth and behind him is a naos containing a standing figure of Re-Harakhte. Between the two boats is a pedestal double the normal height on which, facing to the right, a human-headed sphinx representing Horus the Behdetite tramples on some human beings. It is obvious that the boat of the Harpooner is towing the boat of the gods and the pedestal and the sphinx must be interpreted as being on land close to the water.

Relief 12. On the left the ceremonial bark of Horus the Behdetite faces two pedestals. On the first pedestal, nearest the boat, is a naos in which is seated Horus the Behdetite. The second pedestal supports no less than three naoi: the central naos contains a damaged mummiform figure (apparently unnamed but possibly Ptah) and is flanked to left and right by the shrines of Upper and Lower Egypt, whose doors are apparently shut and bolted.

It is evident that in the Legend of the Winged Disk the pedestals vary considerably in size and nature. Some are small and support a single figure or a single naos; others support a group of figures in action, or a group of figures and a naos, or even three naoi. Superficially, at least, some of them are closer in appearance to the mediaeval Scaffolds than any pedestal in The Triumph of Horus.

These facts raise a very serious question. If we are correct in suggesting that the pedestals in *The Triumph of Horus* supported individual actors in the play, ought we to assume that the same criterion should indicate that the Legend of the Winged Disk was also a play? No convincing answer to this question is possible at present.

If the Legend of the Winged Disk was a play, it certainly was not part of *The Triumph of Horus* from which in every respect it was totally different. The short lines of texts above the figures in the reliefs contain only names and epithets of the figures but not a single spoken word. Apart from the King in Relief 5 (fig. 18), there is not a single word or line of speech attached to any of the figures in the reliefs. Admittedly, it would be possible to present the Main Text in a dramatic form, but it would be a strange form: in each section there are very few named speaking parts; most of the figures depicted in the reliefs are not mentioned in the Main Text nor do they have speeches assigned to them; the greater part of the Main Text is pure narrative; these narrative sections could just conceivably be assigned to a Reader but it must be emphasised that they comprise at least 75 per cent of the whole text. Some possible explanations spring to mind, but to establish them would demand so much research and would lead us so far from our immediate theme that we must content ourselves with presenting the bare facts and leave discussion and the solution of the problem to another occasion.

This discussion has been lengthy but necessary, for it has revealed hitherto unsuspected aspects of drama in Ancient Egypt. It has demonstrated that in the presentation of *The Triumph of Horus* a very simple form of multiple stage was employed, the principal actors, at least, being placed on low pedestals, most of which were quite small, and all apparently being unscreened. Although we may imagine that some of the actors remained on their pedestals throughout the play, our discussion has enabled us to deduce that there must have been a certain amount of movement and that on occasion actors could and did descend from their pedestals to act their parts on or before the Sacred Lake in the centre of the stage. It has also enabled us to suggest with greater confidence a possible stage-setting.

Our discussion has also demonstrated that pedestals were used as well in the Legend of the Winged Disk, that they were larger, more complex and more varied than those of *The Triumph of Horus*, and some may even feel that they have distant resemblances to the mediaeval

Scaffolds. Our knowledge of the true nature of the Legend of the Winged Disk is so imperfect that to attempt to theorise, still less to present firm conclusions, would be unwise and unjustified.

It may, perhaps, be argued that the pedestals in *The Triumph of Horus* are an embryonic form of the mediaeval Scaffolds. But that does not yet justify us in claiming either that there was a link between the two or that the Scaffold evolved from or was inspired by the Edfu pedestal. There does not appear, for instance, to be any comparable feature in the Greek or Roman stage. The arrangement of the pedestals at Edfu was, it would seem, quite different from that of the Scaffolds of the mediaeval theatre in the round which was the starting point of this discussion. The analogy, if analogy there be, is more likely to be sought in the arrangement of the 'houses' or 'mansions' of the passion plays of Valenciennes and Mons: these 'houses' were arranged either in a semi-circle (which was scarcely possible at Edfu) or in a line along a raised platform. Connections and origins are seductive and deceptive concepts. We are dealing with products of the human mind and human beings faced with similar situations are often prone, independently, to react in much the same way to much the same situation. Nevertheless, it is not without interest or importance to be able to record the strong probability that a form of multiple stage was already in use over 2,000 years ago in Ancient Egypt.

Appendix B

The Cheltenham Production of 'The Triumph of Horus'

In 1969 Miss Jennifer Etherington, a member of the staff of the Department of English at St Mary's College, Cheltenham, directed the first modern production of *The Triumph of Horus*. Miss Etherington had been given a copy of the script virtually the same as that later given to Padgate; for several years before she went to Cheltenham she had attended my extra-mural classes in Liverpool, and she had recently had the advantage of a short trip to Egypt. Circumstances prevented any collaboration or consultation between us during the time that Miss Etherington was working on her production and her work was at all times completely unknown to the staff and students at Padgate. Both productions were thus completely independent. At my request Miss Etherington has very kindly sent me the notes on her work which are printed below.

I first took the play as it was and armed a group within the College with it as a Drama Project. They divided into four smaller groups and studied:

1. *Movement.* This was performed in a very stylised and almost dance-like sequence of mobile tableaux with the ritual killing of the hippo resembling somewhat the pattern of an Aztec war-dance. Processional pageant moved the episodes into each other to give continuity and progression and we based the movement motif on the mediaeval mime and gesture symbolism used in religious Mystery and Miracle Plays.

2. *Music.* They studied wall paintings mainly for this. Instruments used were Nordic lyres; Celtic harp—to represent strings of more elaborate harps; horns (posting and one French horn) for bucinas and trumpets; flutes and recorders for the pipes; drums which we assumed they must have used. Out of this came a strange sound which was both dramatic and majestic, and at times sweet and haunting. We augmented the percussion with bells and Chinese cymbals to lend a more marked beat where drums were not used.

3. *Costume.* Again they used books and pictures for reference. Most figures were masked and costume was exaggerated for the same visual

reasons as the Greeks—distance etc. They were improvised by using hessian, paper-sculptured masks and collars and a fair amount of laminated polystyrene which we would not have used in wealthier circumstances. Paint and dye was mainly sprayed to save time. We did this on £10.

4. *Vocal.* They decided that, as the Greeks, Indians, Chinese, etc., the voice was used as a singing rather than speaking instrument. Acoustics in the open or temple forecourt would not take in the spoken word. So we half-sang, half-intoned the words, using choral speech as well as solo and using echoed effects and hummed undertones to heighten or emphasise certain passages. I had a recording of an Aztec lament which helped them to pitch the voice down the nose for the intoning (as in Church).

We performed this as an experiment for some students and mainly for some secondary sixth-formers, who found it a most interesting and surprising experience. It was so totally different from British drama as they knew it that many found it *avant garde* and rather frightening because the characters sounded 'inhuman and unearthly' (to quote) or they described it as an 'ultra-sophisticated kind of musical'.

The *other* thing we did was really more geared to the lower secondary age range and was done with a mixture of students and children. I made a Shadow Theatre (life-size) 92 x 48-inch screen and we performed it in the 'Siamese Method' with giant, mobile puppets in card and tissue cut-out with acetate, and coloured lighting. This was in fact very beautiful and moving in comparison to the physical drama of the other, which was aggressive and often sharply violent in its impact. We used speaking voices, narrator, choruses and more conventional 'mood' music for this but the chief advantage was the complete range of elaboration we were able to use on costumes. Paper, card and wooden struts cost very little and if you know the Shadow Theatres of Thailand and Persia you will understand how beautiful one can make the silhouettes. We emphasised the story element much more and gave the characters more personality for the sake of the age-range of the audience.

Two Bachelor of Education students working on the beginnings of drama last year found 'Horus' most interesting in pushing yet another key into the slot of primitive stage technique and early vocal communication. It has a dynamic quality of both simple and direct statement and a clear-cut beauty of form.

J.E.

Notes

CHAPTER 1

1 Herodotus II, 63 (Rawlinson's translation). *Cf* Hartwig Altenmüller 'Letopolis und die Bericht des Herodot über Papremis' in *Journal Ex Oriente Lux* 18, 271–9.

2 Cairo J. d'E. 85932, lines 5–9, published by E. Drioton, 'Les Fêtes de Bouto' in *Bulletin de l'Institut d'Egypte* 25 (1943), 1–19.

3 Berlin 1204, lines 16–21: H. Schäfer, *Die Mysterien des Osiris in Abydos unter Sesostris III* (Leipzig 1904).

4 K. Sethe, *Dramatische Texte zu altägyptischen Mysterienspielen*: I *Das Denkmal memphitischer Theologie der Schabakostein des Britischen Museems* (1928); II *Der dramatische Ramesseumspapyrus* (1929).

5 H. Junker, *Die Götterlehre von Memphis* (Berlin 1939); *Die politische Lehre von Memphis* (Berlin 1941).

6 Wolfgang Helck, 'Bemerkungen zum Ritual des Dramatischen Ramesseumspapyrus' in *Orientalia* 23 (1954), 383–411.

7 Hartwig Altenmüller, 'Zur Lesung und Deutung des Dramatischen Ramesseumspapyrus' in *Journal Ex Oriente Lux* 19, 421–42.

8 A. de Buck in H. Frankfort, *The Cenotaph of Seti I at Abydos* I, pp. 82–6; II, pls. LXXIV, LXXV.

9 Eberhard Otto, *Das ägyptische Mundöffnungsritual*, 2 vols. (Wiesbaden 1960). A recent translation in French, with brief introduction, in J.-C. Goyon, *Rituels funéraires de l'Ancienne Egypte* (Paris 1972), pp. 87–182.

10 Joachim Spiegel, 'Das Auferstehungsritual der Unas Pyramide' in *Annales du Service des Antiquités de l'Egypte* 53 (1953), 339–439.

11 Joachim Spiegel, *Das Auferstehungsritual der Unas Pyramide* (Wiesbaden 1971).

12 Hartwig Altenmüller, *Die Texte zum Begräbnisritual in den Pyramiden des Alten Reiches* (Wiesbaden 1972).

13 E. Drioton, *Le Théâtre égyptien* (Editions de la Revue du Caire, Cairo 1942).

14 E. Drioton, 'Le Théâtre dans l'Ancienne Egypte' in *Revue de la Societé d'Histoire du Théâtre* 6 (1954), 7–45.

15 Edward Stirling in J. C. Trewin, *The Pomping Folk*. I owe this quotation to my daughter Jennifer.

16 A. de Buck, *The Egyptian Coffin Texts* II, 209c–226a.

17 Book of the Dead, ch. 78. Earliest version, A. de Buck, *op. cit.* IV, 68–86.

Cf A. de Buck, 'The Earliest Version of the Book of the Dead 78' in *Journal of Egyptian Archaeology* 35 (1949), 87–97.

18 Book of the Dead, ch. 39; E. Naville, *Das ägyptische Todtenbuch* II, 107–10 (Berlin 1886).

19 Metternich Stela, lines 48–71; C. E. Sander-Hansen, *Die Texte der Metternichstele* (Copenhagen 1956), 35–40.

20 Metternich Stela, lines 71–83; C. E. Sander-Hansen, *op. cit.*, 43–4.

21 Metternich Stela, lines 168–248a; C. E. Sander-Hansen, *op. cit.*, 60–70.

22 S. Schott, *Urkunden mythologischen Inhalts* (Leipzig 1929), 4–59.

23 Pap. Bremner-Rhind, 33, 1–5; R. O. Faulkner, *The Papyrus Bremner-Rhind* (British Museum no. 10188) = *Bibliotheca Aegyptiaca* III (Brussels 1933), 92–3, and see *Journal of Egyptian Archaeology* 24 (1938), 53.

24 C. Desroches-Noblecourt, 'Le Théâtre égyptien' in *Journal des Savants*, oct.-déc. 1943, 174–5.

25 Pap. Ebers 69, 3–4.

26 Pap. Chester Beatty III, 10, 10–15.

27 *Cf* B. Van de Walle, 'Les origines égyptiennes du théâtre' in *Chronique d'Egypte* 5 (1930), 37–50, and his modified view 'A propos d'un drame égyptien', *loc. cit.*, 214–18. See also A. Klasens, *A Magical Statue Base (Socle Behague) in the Museum of Antiquities at Leiden* (Leiden 1952), 65–6, 82.

28 These versions, in chronological order, are: L. Speleers, *Textes des cercueils du Moyen égyptien*, 80–2, 367–71; J. G. Griffiths, *The Conflict of Horus and Seth* (Liverpool 1960), 52–3; R. O. Faulkner, 'The Pregnancy of Isis' in *Journal of Egyptian Archaeology* 54 (1968), 40–4; Maria Münster, *Untersuchungen zur Gottin Isis* (Berlin 1968), 5–12; M. Gilula, 'Coffin Texts Spell 148' in *Journal of Egyptian Archaeology* 57 (1971), 14–19.

29 Jaroslav Černý, 'Stela of Emhab from Tell Edfou' in *Mitteilungen des Deutschen Archäologischen Instituts, Abt. Kairo* 24 (1969), 87–92.

CHAPTER 2

1 *Journal of Egyptian Archaeology* 21 (1935), 26–7.

2 H. W. Fairman, 'The Myth of Horus at Edfu—I' in *Journal of Egyptian Archaeology* 21 (1935), 26–36.

3 *Journal of Egyptian Archaeology* 21 (1935), 26.

4 E. Drioton, 'Nouveaux fragments de théâtre égyptien' in *La Revue du Caire* 107 (1948), 457–88; reprinted in his *Pages d'Egyptologie* (Cairo 1957), 331–62.

5 E. Drioton, *Le Texte dramatique d'Edfou* (*Cahiers des Annales du Service des Antiquités de l'Egypte* 11, Cairo 1948).

6 E. Chassinat, *Le Temple d'Edfou* III, 28, 12; 257, 15.

7 E. Chassinat, *Le Temple d'Edfou* VI, 186, 12–190, 11.

8 E. Chassinat, *Le Temple d'Edfou* VI, 14,12–13.

9 Line 3, No. 8: *cf* H. Schäfer, *Ein Bruchstück altägyptischer Annalen* (Berlin 1902).

10 T. Säve-Söderbergh, *On Egyptian Representations of Hippopotamus Hunting as a Religious Motive* (=*Horae Soederblomianae* III, Uppsala 1950).

11 K. Sethe, *Die altägyptische Pyramidentexte* §235. *Cf* also §§1211–1212 which also refer to the cutting off of the heads of *sabet*-snakes which forms the Interlude in Act I, Scene iv.

12 A. de Buck, *The Egyptian Coffin Texts* I, 259a–c.

13 N. de Garis Davies and A. H. Gardiner, *The Tomb of Amenemhet* (London 1915), 28–30.

14 Papyrus Chester Beatty I. A. H. Gardiner, *The Library of A. Chester Beatty: The Chester Beatty Papyri, No. 1* (Oxford 1931).

15 C. Desroches-Noblecourt, *Tutankhamen* (London 1963), pl. XLV, p. 217; The British Museum, *Treasures of Tutankhamun* (London 1972), no. 27.

16 M. Alliot, *Le Culte d'Horus à Edfou au temps des Ptolémées* (Cairo 1954), II, 468 and n. 2.

17 The positions of some of the tombs are marked in the plan in M. Alliot, *Rapport sur les fouilles de Tell Edfou (1933)*, pl. XX.

18 E. Chassinat, *Le Temple d'Edfou* IV, 3,1–8.

19 The term employed by Fecht has been adopted here. As defined here 'colon' differs slightly from its application to ancient Greek verse. Professor Fecht's principal studies are: 'Die Wiedergewinnung der altägyptischen Verskunst' in *Mitteilungen des Deutschen Archäologischen Instituts, Abt. Kairo* 19 (1963), 54–96; 'Die Form der altägyptischen Literatur: Metrische und stylistische Analayse' in *Zeitschrift für Ägyptische Sprache* 91 (1964), 11–63; 92 (1965), 10–32; *Literarische Zeugnisse zur 'Persönlichen Frömmigkeit' in Ägypten* (Heidelberg 1965), especially pp. 13–38. See also his *Wortakzent und Silbenstruktur* (Gluckstadt 1960).

APPENDIX A

1 E. Chassinat, *Le Temple d'Edfou* IX, pls. 69–73.

2 E. Chassinat, *Le Temple de Dendara* III, pl. 190.

3 E. Chassinat and F. Daumas, *Le Temple de Dendara* V, pl. 404; VI, pls. 504; 512.

4 F. Daumas, *Les Mammisis de Dendara*, pls. 60 bis; 71.

5 *Cf* for example, E. Chassinat, *Le Temple d'Edfou* IX, pl. 30a; X, pl. 151.

6 Glynne Wickham, *Early English Stages* I, 81 (Routledge, 1959).